Finding The Few

Dedication

To Sgt Pilot Hubert Hastings Adair
Missing 6 November 1940
Denied a last resting place by circumstances and events

Finding The Few

Some Outstanding Mysteries of the Battle of Britain
Investigated and Solved

Andy Saunders

Grub Street • London

Published by
Grub Street Publishing
4 Rainham Close
London
SW11 6SS

British Library Cataloguing in Publication Data

Saunders, Andy.
  Finding the few : some outstanding mysteries of the
  Battle of Britain investigated and solved.
  1. Britain, Battle of, Great Britain, 1940 – Biography.
  2. World War, 1939-1945 – Aerial operations, British.
  3. World War, 1939-1945 – Missing in action – Great Britain.
  4. Air pilots, Military – Great Britain – Biography.
  I. Title
  940.5'44'941'0922-dc22

  ISBN-13: 9781906502553

Design by Roy Platten, Eclipse, Hemel Hempstead
roy.eclipse@btopenworld.com

Printed and bound by the MPG Books Group

Grub Street Publishing uses only FSC
(Forest Stewardship Council) paper for its books

Contents

Acknowledgements

MANY FRIENDS and colleagues have assisted greatly in my writing of this book. Without them all this tribute to some of Churchill's Few could not have been written. In no particular order of merit I should like to thank the following:

Mark Kirby, Peter Cornwell, Steve Brew, Robin Hill, Dave Smith, Keith Dowle, Winston Ramsey, Paul Cole, Ruth Bloom, Chris Goss, Alfred Price, Andrew Sherwood, Ken Rimmel, Peter Dimond, Steve Vizard, John Ellis, Pat Burgess, Howard Pearce, Terry Thompson, Ian Hutton, Denis Knight, Dean Sumner, Geoffrey and Bolly Gilders, Joan Worth, Lt Cdr Worth, Steve Hall, Philippa Hodgkiss (now Wheeler), Richard Smith, Norman Franks, Dave Ross, Dave Buchanan, K D Clarke, John Elgar-Whinney, Richard Hukins, Carol Ventura, Rene Hukin, Jennifer Fergus, Robyn Fergus, Martyn Cully, Mark Wenbourne, Simon Muggleton, Amira Soliman, Geoff Nutkins, Colin Brown, Simon Parry, Ken Wynn, Gerry Burke, Dick Walker, Peter Halton, Steve Whitehorn, Wojtek Matusiak, Danny Burt and the late Peter Foote, Alan Brown and Andy Cresswell.

I should also like to thank John Davies and his understanding and efficient team at Grub Street Publishing for making this book possible and for working with me under sometimes difficult conditions.

Last, but by no means least, a big thank you to Zoe who has endured me shutting myself away and being sometimes rather un-communicative as I put all this together or travelled hither and thither to meet and interview people or to spend long hours away at the National Archives in Kew. Thank you, Zoe.

If I have left anyone out, then I extend my sincerest apologies to you. It is a purely unintentional oversight on my part. Thank you one and all.

Foreword

Tony G Pickering

THERE ARE many stories dealing with the operational exploits of wartime aircrew that have been written since the end of the 1939-45 war. However, comparatively little has been recorded about those members of RAF Fighter Command lost during the Battle of Britain and who were officially reported as missing. They were usually very young, perhaps only 19 or 20 years of age, and with little or no combat experience. They were given a name on the Runnymede Memorial or, if an unidentified body were found, they were buried under a Commonwealth War Graves Commission headstone bearing the inscription "Known unto God". Probably due to the operational demands being made on us aircrew at the time we gave little or no thought to our comrades who had been lost and not found. In any event, there was a war to be getting on with and it was really not good to dwell too much on our lost pals. Maybe we of such a young age just believed that senior officers would take care of things and ensure that no effort would be spared to find and identify our friends. Little did we know.

My experience of these tragic losses in 1940 relates to my time on 501 Squadron. I knew three of these young fliers on the squadron – two of whom were later identified and given correct CWGC headstones. One of them, however, is still classified as 'missing'.

I feel that sincere appreciation must go to those members of the research and recovery teams who, at considerable personal expense, have spent time and energy investigating the crash sites of some of these missing men with a high degree of success. I was very personally involved in the Eddie Egan case which is covered in this book. I was flying alongside Eddie in his final combat and later became involved in the investigation of the story by the press and so many years after I had seen my comrade-in-arms disappear I was at last able to attend his military funeral at Brookwood Cemetery. Eddie and I had been friends and had shared our off-duty times together. I had often thought about him over the years and wondered what had become of him. Finally to know was very important to me.

There is no doubt at all that success in ascertaining Eddie's location was due solely to the work carried out by enthusiastic researchers who were determined that Eddie should be found, laid to rest and his story finally told. I am certain that many will appreciate this opportunity to read of the efforts made by these researchers and historians and to be able to see the detailed extent of their invaluable work. It is work that has been often overlooked and often criticised. Were it not for the tireless dedication of some of these researchers the last resting places of these unfortunate young fighter pilots from 1940 would not be known today. As a former Battle of Britain pilot, and one who has been touched by the fruits of their labours, I offer my sincerest thanks. I am sure they are sentiments that would be echoed by Eddie Egan and all of the other valiant souls whose stories are told in the following pages.

Tony G Pickering

Tony G Pickering
Sgt Pilot. 501 Squadron. August – December 1940
RAF Stations Kenley & Gravesend

Introduction

I N 1972 the wreckage of a Hurricane aircraft was uncovered at Goudhurst in Kent from the place where it had been shot down during the Battle of Britain. In the cockpit were the mortal remains of Pilot Officer George James Drake, a young South African fighter pilot who had been posted 'missing' after being shot down during an air battle over the Mayfield area on 9th September 1940. The recovery team were taken aback by their discovery and both national and local news media reacted with equal astonishment at this grim and sad discovery. That a fighter pilot shot down during the Battle of Britain could still be missing with no known grave and within the British Isles was surely highly unusual. Certainly the Ministry of Defence thought so. Writing to the recovery team shortly after the discovery the ministry were clear that this was a unique discovery. A one-off, in fact. As things would eventually turn out it was far from the case.

Research carried out across the 1970s and 1980s revealed that quite a number of Battle of Britain pilots who had been lost in 1940 still rested at the crash sites of their aircraft strewn across south-east England. To the author it seemed astonishing that members of Churchill's 'Few', perhaps nationally revered above all war heroes, should lie forgotten in scattered and unmarked graves. Somehow there was something inherently wrong that such a situation should exist – the more so because determined research by amateur enthusiasts and historians could reveal their whereabouts. All the while the authorities had, in effect, washed their hands of these cases and blandly stated that their responsibility towards those casualties had been discharged by placing their names on the Runnymede Memorial. Meanwhile, relatives and friends who were still living often yearned for some knowledge about what had become of loved ones. Even after the passage of many decades this knowledge is of huge importance to those affected. Indeed, as this book is being written there are at least two daughters of 'missing' Battle of Britain pilots still alive. Both were born after the deaths of their respective fathers. The knowledge as to what happened to both of their fathers has been of incalculable personal significance more than sixty years on. Such information was finally imparted to them by civilian researchers and not by the authorities.

The stories told in this book are, of their very nature, both sad and tragic. Such is the result of war. The human cost of lives lost, and of lives left behind and shattered, is almost incomprehensible to those not directly affected. Some of the stories do not exactly reflect much glory or credit on the authorities. Equally, some throw up questions about the propriety, actions or motivation of some of those involved with those recoveries – although all such recoveries, with the passage of time, are of themselves now historic events. All of them, though, hide accounts of heroism and patriotic duty in the face of overwhelming odds. Whatever the side-issues related to the recovery of these airmen might have been, whatever the controversies that have arisen, the important issue here is that these men have, one way or another, finally found a proper resting place. To many it is only right that the 'Few' are thus honoured.

Andy Saunders
East Sussex, March 2009

CHAPTER 1

First On The List

THE FIRST name to be found on the official Battle of Britain Roll is that of Sgt Pilot Hubert Hastings Adair of 213 Squadron. In all published lists, on the Roll of Honour at Westminster Abbey and on the magnificent Battle of Britain Memorial on the Thames Embankment at Westminster Sgt Adair's name is the first, alphabetically, to be found. It is therefore fitting that he should also be the first RAF casualty dealt with in detail within these pages. Not only is his name the first on the list of the RAF's serving Battle of Britain aircrew but he is also one of those still classified as 'missing'. That said, his date of death was outside the official period of the Battle of Britain (10 July-31 October 1940) but his inclusion here will surely be seen as both significant and appropriate. His 'qualification' for inclusion within the limited criteria set for this book is threefold. First, he was a participant in the Battle of Britain. Second, he was posted as missing in action over the UK and, thirdly, his status continues to be classified as such – notwithstanding the almost certain discovery of his bodily remains in the wreckage of a Hurricane fighter during 1979.

Sgt Hubert Hastings Adair of 213 Squadron was lost flying from RAF Tangmere on 6 November 1940. Despite the recovery of his Hurricane in the 1970's and extensive research he remains "missing" to this day.

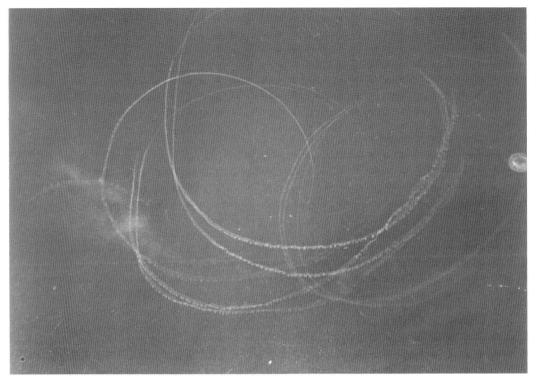

On 6 November 1940 Hubert Adair was shot down in a short sharp battle over the Solent area. Remarkably, local schoolboy Alexander McKee snapped the vapour trails formed during that very battle from his back garden.

Teenagers Colin and Alexander McKee were keen observers of the air battles that raged around them in skies over their Hampshire home during 1940 but it was the young Alexander who enthusiastically recorded what he saw and heard during that momentous period. In his diaries, meticulously preserved post-war, Alexander had not only described in words the sights and sounds of battle but had also made sketches and watercolour paintings of some of those events. Incredibly, he even recorded some of the battles he saw via the medium of the camera lens and had made use of his limited supply of film to compile a unique perspective of the Battle of Britain through the eyes of one observer. As the aerial fighting of July and August moved on into the autumn so the young Alexander continued his avid recording, and by November he was still enthusiastically logging events. November 6th 1940 was no exception. Writing in his diary the young Alexander recorded:

"Afternoon. Sirens and then gunfire! I spotted many vapour trails over Portchester. There seemed to be several formations. First, came four planes travelling westward towards us under the trails. Two silver specks danced above, and were joined by three more. Trails formed on some of these and eight other planes in compact formation left comet-like trails. Gradually a confused mass of vapour trails like an octopus all tangled up came into being above our heads as the fighters weaved in and out. A plane stood on its ear, another looped, just like a coin spun casually upwards from the fingers. Others whirled around each other in merry circles to the chattering tune of machine guns. Then the sky rained planes. Like leaves in the autumn sky they came to earth. A Hurricane shot over Wallington very fast and at a flat angle to disappear behind the hill. Almost on its heels came another plane falling flat and fast. Neither rose again. My brother Colin then yelled 'Look…he's going straight down. He's into a cloud now. He's doing a terrible speed…' I looked and although I failed to spot the vertical one I did see another plane descending just above the horizon."

Although young Alexander and Colin did not know it they had witnessed the brief and bloody encounter between Me 109s of Helmut Wick's JG2 (the Richthofen Geschwader) and the Hurricanes of 145 and 213 Squadrons up from Tangmere, the Spitfires of 602 Squadron from Westhampnett and Hurricanes of 238 Squadron from Chilbolton. Sgt Adair's 213 Squadron had been ordered up to patrol base and then Portsmouth at 25,000 ft, or 'Angels 25' in RAF parlance. It was here, over Portsmouth, that the fatal encounter with the Me 109s took place – the Messerschmitts led into action by the enigmatic Luftwaffe ace Major Helmut Wick in an event that was detailed in a book called *Helmut Wick – Das Leben Eines Fliegerhelden (Helmut Wick – The Life of a Flying Hero)* by Josef Grabler and published in Germany during 1941. Heavily laden with more than just overtones of wartime propaganda the book must be viewed in that context, although specific episodes are carefully recorded in considerable detail. Such is the case in relation to the events of 6 November 1940 and Wick's account of that day's fighting provides a fascinating comparison with how things were viewed from the ground by the two McKee boys.

"Today we had a terrific time again. We meet a heap of Hurricanes which fly lower than we do. I am just getting ready to attack when I notice something above me and I immediately shout over the intercom 'Attention! Spitfires above us!' But they were so far away that I could begin attacking the Hurricanes. They were just turning away from their original course and that sealed their fate. Almost simultaneously the four of us fired at their formation. One went on my account. The rest of the Hurricanes moved away, but then pulled up to a higher altitude. During this manoeuvre I once again caught the one on the outer right hand side. He was done for immediately, and went straight down! Now I can't say what it was that was the matter with me on this day, November 6. I wasn't sure if I wasn't well or if it was my nerves which were about to break. When my second Englishman was prone down below I just wanted to go home.

"I would have had enough fuel for a few more minutes, but the urge to go home completely overwhelmed me. Also, to justify myself – if that is at all necessary – there wasn't much I could do with the few minutes I had left in reserve. As we begin to turn away and we are holding the course for home I spot below me three Spitfires. I am the first to see them and attack immediately. Already the first one falls! But now I say to myself 'Go for the others!' – if I let the other two get away they will probably shoot down my comrades tomorrow!"

Wick goes on to record his return flight across the Channel and a triumphal arrival back home when he noted to himself that the day's 'bag' had taken him to 53 victories and that he had only one more claim to make before catching up with his old fighter instructor,

Werner Mölders. *(In fact, post-war research indicates that Wick's tally at the day's-end was probably 52 rather than 53.)*

Clearly, and with the tactical advantage of height, Wick's Messerschmitts had first fallen on the Hurricanes of 145 and 213 Squadrons and in a sharp and bloody encounter had bludgeoned two Hurricanes from these squadrons out of the sky. Up from Chilbolton, 238 Squadron had also joined the fray and one of their Hurricanes, too, was sent crashing to earth under the collective cannonade of JG2. The Spitfires of 602 Squadron, though, had fared rather better and came through unscathed. Indeed, and to partly redress the balance, Sgt A McDowall had sent Ofw Heinrich Klopp of 5/JG2 into the sea off Bonchurch on the Isle of Wight in his Me 109 E-4, 'Black 1' W.Nr 2751. Of 602 Squadron's participation in this action, and as a counter-point to Wick's contemporary narrative, we have the first-hand diary account of 602's commanding officer, Squadron Leader 'Sandy' Johnstone. He wrote:

> "Was busy dealing with a mountain of bumff in the office when a call came for the whole squadron to scramble, so I dropped everything and dashed off to lead it, as it was ages since we had had one of these! In the event, we intercepted about thirty 109s approaching the Isle of Wight but when they saw us approaching they scarpered, making no attempt to stay and fight it out. However I am pleased to say that McDowall got one as it scooted rapidly uphill. I saw it go down in flames. Some Hurricanes from Tangmere also arrived on the scene when Mac and one of the 213 boys were able to claim a second victory between them, but I did not witness that one as I was too busy trying to catch up with another 109 which was outpacing me in the climb. Lord Trenchard had been right. The Germans are behaving like a bunch of cissies!"

Again, we have here a fascinating first hand account of the action over the Solent area that day from another perspective. However, Johnstone's remark about the Germans turning and running for home and behaving like cissies is actually rather wide of the mark and more than a little unfair on the Luftwaffe fighter pilots. We know that the Germans fought hard and well in that action and had achieved a creditable score of victories to prove so – and that is notwithstanding Wick's surprisingly candid openness about his attack of nerves. What Johnstone probably did not realise was that the Messerschmitt 109s really had no choice other than to turn for home so quickly since they were already at the limit of their range. Fuel reserves after their brief combat were already running low for the long flight home over the sea. Indeed, so desperately short was Helmut Wick's fuel on his return from this combat operation that he was unable to carry out the customary victory rolls over his home airfield.

Major Helmut Wick, one of the three top German aces who accounted for RAF pilots covered in this book.

Despite Wick's assertion that he had downed at least one of Johnstone's Spitfires (his actual claims for the combat show three Spitfires downed), this was not the case and either he incorrectly believed he had shot down some of the Spitfires or, more likely, had misidentified his Hurricane victims as Spitfires in the heat of battle. Either way, JG2 over-claimed in this action with a reported tally of eight destroyed – five Hurricanes and three Spitfires. If we count one Hurricane of 145 Squadron that made a forced-landing back at Tangmere after combat with the Messerschmitts over the Isle of Wight, then JG2's tally can only be made to reach a maximum of four. In reality, just three fell over the actual combat zone. That said, though, there can be little doubting that all of the Hurricanes were downed by the guns of JG2 with Major Wick, Oblt Leie and Oblt Hahn all making claims around the Southampton and Isle of Wight area in this combat and with Wick claiming two Hurricanes and three Spitfires, Leie getting two Hurricanes and Hahn another Hurricane. Who shot down who it is impossible to say, especially given the element of over-claiming by the German pilots. What is certain though is that one of the victims of that combat was Sgt Hubert Adair who failed to return to his Tangmere base after the encounter. Very clearly 'Paddy' Adair must have been one of the fighters seen to fall by the brothers McKee and by a process of elimination, and by examining the known details of the other RAF fighter losses that day, it is possible positively to ascertain where his Hurricane fell. Again, we turn to Alexander's diary for that clue:

"We found a woman who had bussed past a burning plane near Widley and sure enough there in a field below the road a group of tin-hatted men stood around a white gash in the soil. Overhead, where battle had raged shortly beforehand, a Hawker Hart circled around, just like a vulture floating round a corpse. I biked through a field and turned the glasses onto a small elongated tangle of silver and green metal. In most places it wasn't more than six inches high. Smoke drifted faintly away on the wind. Twenty yards was the nearest I managed to get. One chap had seen it come down. He said it had been a Hurricane and simply dived in under full throttle at about 500mph. An ambulance stood waiting for the soldiers to pull the pilot out but the smouldering heap was too hot to touch. Small boys, though, collected bits of metal and their pockets bulged!"

What Alexander McKee had witnessed on the hill above Widley was clearly the aftermath of the vertical crash his brother Colin had seen. Who though was the pilot? From all available evidence it was clear that the unfortunate occupant had died in his Hurricane and with the established knowledge that there were only three contenders for Hurricane losses that day then there was, at least, a starting point. Of these three, however, only two were found to have known burial places. The same two could also be tied to specific crash locations. First, we have Sgt J K Haire of 145 Squadron who was shot down and killed at Heasley Farm, Arreton, on the Isle of Wight and who was taken home for burial in his native Ulster at Belfast (Dundonald) Cemetery and then we have Fg Off James Tillet of 238 Squadron who was killed when his Hurricane crashed and burnt out at Park Gate, Fareham. Tillet was taken the short distance to Anns Hill Cemetery, Gosport, for burial thus leaving only one other casualty, Sgt Hubert Adair, to consider. Of Adair, no trace had evidently been found and he was thus commemorated by name on Panel 11 of the Runnymede Memorial to the RAF's missing. The conclusion is obvious; the body of the unfortunate Adair has never been recovered although by a process of simple deduction, his *must* have been the

Hurricane that slammed with such awful ferocity into the chalk hill at Widley.

In 1979, and armed with Alexander McKee's accounts, the author set out to find anyone in the Widley area who might offer more clues as to what had happened. The search did not take long. The crash was established to have happened at Pigeon House Farm and here by an incredible stroke of good fortune were found to be living Robert and Ernest Ware – two brothers who had farmed the land for the Southwick & Roche Court Estates Company since before the war. Like the McKee brothers they too had seen the battle and subsequent crash and their recall was equally vivid. The noise of the approaching aircraft was so tremendous that Robert flung himself under a farm cart for some measure of safety and, peering out, he watched as the Hurricane smashed into the field just 200 yards away shaking the ground underneath him "like an earthquake". As it hit, a huge column of smoke, dirt and debris shot skywards and then, seemingly in slow motion, cascaded back to earth in a massive arc.

For several days the wreckage burnt underground until finally the Ware brothers were instructed to clear up the scattered debris and fill in the crater. Both were adamant in 1979 that no attempt was ever made to recover the pilot. Here then was the last resting place of Sgt Adair. Further confirmation, if any were needed, that the pilot was not recovered was provided by a former officer of the 35th Anti-Aircraft Brigade stationed at Fareham who told how a Royal Air Force officer arrived on the scene from Tangmere and searched amongst the debris where he found the aircraft serial number. This, he told the army officer, would enable the aircraft and its pilot to be identified and if true then the number the unknown officer found would have been V7602. Again if true, the RAF at Tangmere would have had clear evidence pointing to what had happened to Adair and exactly where he had crashed.

Whilst it might seem surprising that no further action was taken, it will be seen later in this book that this would not have been the first time that a crash location of a missing pilot had been found, clearly identified and then abandoned. One can only speculate as to why that might have been. It was not, however, a situation that was to endure entirely unchanged in the case of Sgt Adair and the Widley crash.

With the increase of 'aviation archaeology' in the 1970s and 1980s, the site at Widley came under scrutiny by the then Wealden Aviation Archaeological Group who were keen to follow up on the author's research and carry out an investigative excavation at the site. At this time, in 1979, there were no legislative restrictions imposed upon such recoveries and no requirement to seek a licence for recovery from the Ministry of Defence. Such requirements were not imposed until the implementation of the Protection of Military Remains Act in 1986 and in the case of the Widley site no MOD licence would have been forthcoming after 1986 by virtue of the fact that human remains might well still be present. Therefore, and armed with the author's research and with Alexander McKee and the Ware brothers all present, the Wealden group located and excavated the crash site on 6 October 1979 – the spot having been pin-pointed with precision by Bob Ware. After all, being just two hundred yards from a crash like this was clearly something that anyone would recall with indelible clarity! As for the Wealden group, their purpose and intent was clear; recover and identify the wreck and find its pilot in order that this missing airman could be satisfactorily accounted for.

Despite impact with the chalky hills the wreckage was found to have driven itself almost ten feet into the hard ground – testimony to the awful ferocity of the crash. Not surprisingly the surviving wreckage was twisted and contorted almost beyond recognition and the subsequent fire and the situation of the wreckage in water-permeable chalk had done little to enhance the state of preservation. Even the mighty Rolls-Royce Merlin engine was smashed to pieces with valves and con-rods mangled into S-shapes and the huge forging of the crankshaft twisted like a banana. Alexander McKee, present throughout the excavation, was himself a military historian, writer and archaeologist and had already achieved fame through his then recent discovery of the Tudor warship *Mary Rose*. As such, he was well placed to be an objective observer of the excavations unfolding in front of him as he re-lived the events he had witnessed way back in 1940. His notes, just as his wartime diary, remain as a further historical record in their own right of the story of the Widley Hurricane crash and of Sgt Adair. He wrote:

"The team moved so fast, so surely and so expertly that I was hard pressed to keep up. The first excavation was filled in after removal of top soil had brought to light only small scattered bits of dural. The dig moved slightly and initial removal of topsoil produced some bigger bits indicating 'mother lode' and then a complete group of four Browning .303 machine guns were found – one wing battery of a Hurricane. Digging slightly NE part of the tail was found, about three feet down, then part of the rudder. Bits of broken armour plate from behind the pilot's seat then parts of the parachute harness, the canvas front of the oxygen mask and the compass badly bent and flattened. Then the gunsight and the D Ring of the ripcord at about the six foot level. Then a buckled spoon. The spoon was curious, I thought. It must have been in the Hurricane. Otherwise, why so drastically bent?

The clues were not long in coming. This is the front of a parachute harness release buckle and the parachute D ring that operated the rip-cord. The presence of these items gave a clear indication that the pilot had not escaped.

"Not surprisingly bones were found at this level. I noticed how quickly the team in the hole spotted the bones and set them carefully aside. Their recognition was much faster than mine but of course I was standing further away and up-top. I do not think they were likely to have missed much. Distinct burn mark stratification in the sides of the dig showed clearly the shape of the crater. Then, at eight to nine feet came the propeller boss after the mangled engine. Then, the four missing guns were found – absolutely vertical with butts uppermost."

Although he could not sneak a photograph of the crash site at Widley where Sgt Adair's Hurricane had crashed, McKee nevertheless recorded the scene in watercolours later that same evening. A RAF Hawker biplane circles the scene which is framed by a rainbow. Tin-hatted soldiers wait around the smoking crater while an army ambulance stands by.

As a contemporary record of what he saw in 1979, McKee's notes make a fascinating adjunct to what he had seen in 1940. Aside from his diary and the photograph, Alexander had also made an almost childishly simple watercolour painting of what he had observed at Widley....the crater, the circling Hawker Hart, a waiting ambulance – all framed by a late afternoon rainbow. Incredibly, an old green ambulance was being used by one of the recovery team as transport and was parked on almost the same spot as the 1940 ambulance giving Alexander a jolt back in time when he arrived on the scene! To have seen the battle in which the aircraft was lost, to have witnessed the crash scene and to have photographed and recorded it all, one way or another, way back in 1940 was remarkable enough but the continuation of that personal link by witnessing and being involved in the recovery of the wreck and its pilot can only be regarded as a unique experience and event. However, the reality of the October 1979 finds now had to be dealt with.

Faced with what were clearly human remains, albeit fragmentary and calcified, the recovery team duly suspended work and notified the Hampshire Police. By early afternoon a large number of police officers had arrived and were swarming all over the field at Pigeon House Farm. Amongst them was HM Coroner's Officer for the district. Incredibly though, and

In 1979 that same site came under investigation by the Wealden Aviation Archaeological Group. Here, a mechanical excavator probes the chalky soil at Pigeon House Farm for clues. This is, broadly, the same view painted by McKee. Coincidentally, an old green military ambulance is being used for the team's transport!

despite a complete news embargo by the team, the police officers were beaten to the field by a journalist clutching his notebook and camera! Quizzed as to how he came to know about the find he answered to an astonished group "Oh… the police have just 'phoned and told me!" Already, and ahead of any formal investigations, the story was in the public domain and by Monday 8 October it had reached both local and national newspapers.

The group remained tight lipped though about the pilot's identity pending the possibility of an inquest and the formal identification and naming of the pilot whose remains had been discovered. There was though a problem with taking this process forward which was, quite simply, that the destruction of both machine and occupant had been total. Almost complete disintegration of the Hurricane had taken place with the high speed and vertical impact with the chalk. The consequential effect upon the unfortunate aeroplane's occupant needs no clarification here, save to say that the added factor of extreme fire and then severe corrosion through water percolation of the wreckage over almost forty years had further destroyed or damaged any evidence of identification – either of the pilot or his Hurricane. In the case of personal identification, no identity discs were found and any paperwork had clearly burnt.

In the case of the aircraft the individual identification of Hurricane V7602 would have been stamped onto a matchbox-sized brass plate secured to the cockpit structure near the fuel cocks *(examples of this data plate will be seen later on in the book)* but despite a thorough search no trace of the data plate was found. Its discovery alone would have been sufficient to identify by name the pilot as Sgt Hubert Hastings Adair 580088. As it was, the coroner's investigating officer was faced with a pretty blank canvas when it came to dealing with who the airman might have been. All that existed was circumstantial evidence as to the date and details of the crash although it has to be said that the evidence amassed by the recovery group was overwhelmingly convincing. Again, we will see later in this book at least one case where another coroner in a different district, faced with a similar set of circumstances, was content to name another set of discovered remains as a specific pilot. Unfortunately this was not to be in the case of the Widley pilot.

As we have seen, the evidence that points to the remains discovered at Pigeon House Farm, Widley, being those

Witness to the 1940 crash had been Bob Ware, who still farmed the land in 1979. Here he examines the chalk encrusted remnants of the Rolls-Royce Merlin engine after excavation. The total destruction of the aeroplane is self evident.

The Hurricane's entire battery of .303 Browning machine guns is laid out alongside the excavation. Each one was found buried vertically in the chalk, the butt end being some twelve inches into the ground.

of Sgt Adair are compelling. Put simply it can be no other pilot and yet, as this book is written, Hubert Adair continues to be listed as missing in action. Why that should be is indeed a curious tale.

Faced with no positive evidence of identification, the coroner elected to hold no inquest since the Ministry of Defence were unable to offer any information to support the case for it being Hubert Adair. Further, the advice of the Ministry of Defence to the coroner was that the matter might best be dealt with by not holding an inquest and simply "disposing" of the remains locally. That said, it is curious to note that the Ministry of Defence had clearly already considered the possibility of the pilot being Sgt Adair and by 22 October 1979 they had notified the coroner that they were unable to trace any next of kin in this case. Further information also emerged from the MOD indicating that their casualty records stated that the wreckage of the Widley Hurricane had burned for three days.

What is significant here is that this specific statement suggests that there was *already* some link in MOD casualty records with Adair and the Widley crash. The note about the burning wreckage would not have been some random file note held by the ministry but some note on the casualty file for Sgt Adair. In other words, the serial number found by the RAF officer in 1940, together with the date and circumstances of the crash must have already been connected to this casualty. Unfortunately, the RAF casualty files are still held by the MOD but are closed to public inspection and therefore any connection made in Sgt Adair's file with Widley has to be only an assumption on the part of the author. It is surely significant though that the MOD *did* attempt to find Adair's relatives and next of kin in 1979. If there had been no link in the minds of the MOD officials between Sgt Adair and the Widley casualty then why else would they have sought to find his family?

Following on from advice by the MOD to the coroner it did turn out to be the case that HM Coroner elected not to hold an inquest. Instead, he ordered that the remains be scattered at Portchester Crematorium and this was duly carried out on 29 October 1979 just three short weeks after their discovery. Officially, the remains were classified as "Unidentified Remains" by the coroner. Officially, too, they were classified as "Unidentified RAF Pilot" by the crematorium when writing to the author in 1983 although rather oddly a letter from the Cemetery & Crematorium Superintendent Mr E C Appleton to the coroner confirming that the remains had been disposed of refers to them as being "the late Hubert Adair". Altogether a perplexing situation and a set of circumstances that ultimately denied Sgt Pilot Adair a named place of burial.

Indeed, the "disposal" of the remains in this way even precluded their burial as an 'Unknown Airman' and totally removed any hope that the emergence of subsequent evidence might allow positive identification later. As we have seen, the MOD failed to locate any family members in 1979 although, had they done so, it is unlikely that any relatives would have been able to throw further light that might enable identification. Worth remembering, too, that this event long pre-dated the use of DNA for identification and thus any investigation using this route was not then available. Seemingly poor old Paddy Adair had not only been lost in 1940 but again in 1979 and all hope to solve the mystery of his disappearance was officially extinguished.

Unhappy at the rather premature and unsatisfactory closure of the case, the author set out in late 1979 to track down any living relatives of Hubert Adair, this attempt notwithstanding the MOD's inability to find anyone during their investigations of October that year. By January 1980, however the author had found and established contact with Adair's surviving sister, Esther Sherwood. By the simple expedient of letters to the press, a number of friends and relatives almost immediately came forward. Esther was sheltered from news appertaining to events at Widley but, nonetheless, came forward with brief biographical details of her elder brother who had been born in 1917, had lived in Grosvenor Road, Norwich, and attended the City of Norwich School in Eaton Road. Two elder brothers had emigrated pre-war to Canada, whilst the sisters remained in England. It also emerged that Hubert had a daughter and both she and her mother were both still living in 1979.

Despite the shock of discovery that might have been caused after so many years it is hard not to believe that, ultimately, the discovery and proper burial of their Paddy would have been a comfort to all members of the family. Some small comfort, though, might be the memorial bearing his name erected close to the crash site by local enthusiast Graham Alderson in the 1990s. There is also another postscript to the saga of the Widley Hurricane.

Photographs of 213 Squadron during 1940 are hard to find and although this group of pilots does not include Sgt Adair, it is taken during the Battle of Britain period at Tangmere.

Also in the 1990s a Hampshire-based researcher of local air-war events, Ian Hutton, considered the possibility that some tiny piece of vital evidence may have been overlooked at Widley during work on the site in 1979. He may well have been right. Perhaps even the small brass aircraft constructor's plate still lay concealed there? Either way, the passage of years since 1979 had seen the introduction of the Protection of Military Remains Act in 1986 and any work on sites such as this one required the granting of a licence by the Ministry of Defence and Ian accordingly applied for authority to work on the site at Pigeon House Farm. It was refused. Ordinarily, permission is now denied where the presence of human remains is suspected but as it was known that a set of remains had already been found here in 1979, the reason for denial of a licence prompts speculation. Given the fact that the discovered remains had been disposed of would it not be awkward if evidence now emerged to prove conclusively who that pilot was?

Of Hubert Adair, surprisingly little is known about his RAF career save that he joined as a direct entry airman under-training pilot in January 1936. From here he eventually flew Fairey Battles in France with 88 Squadron before volunteering for Fighter Command and joining 151 Squadron at Digby on 2 September 1940. By the 16th of that month he had moved to 213 Squadron at Tangmere and earned his spurs as a Battle of Britain pilot, qualifying to be awarded the Battle of Britain Clasp to his 1939-45 Star. On 5 November 1940 Paddy was involved in a night landing accident at Tangmere. Although unhurt it is possible that he had been un-nerved by the experience. Perhaps he had lost his edge when thrown into combat the very next day? This, of course, is pure conjecture. What is not supposition though is that Sgt Hubert Hastings Adair 580088 almost certainly lost his life on 6 November when his Hurricane crashed at Pigeon House Farm, Widley, and was subsequently found in 1979. Today, however, he is still missing.

First to Be Found

WHILST THE Battle of Britain has become ingrained upon British consciousness since those momentous events of 1940, it may well have been the film 'Battle of Britain' that sparked even wider interest in the subject when it was released in 1969. To the film has certainly been attributed the accolade of almost being responsible for the birth of historic aircraft preservation in Britain. That perhaps is hardly surprising given the considerable air force that was assembled to make the film. If nothing else the cinematographic representation of the Battle of Britain was a catalyst for huge enthusiasm in the subject and an interest that spawned a veritable army of aircraft recovery groups intent on salvaging tangible relics of this epic battle. One such was the Ashford and Tenterden Aircraft Recovery Group who later formed the still extant Brenzett Aeronautical Museum.

Pilot Officer George Drake was a South African pilot who flew with 607 Squadron from Tangmere. He was shot down and posted as missing in action on 9 September 1940. It was not until 1972 that his Hurricane was found at Goudhurst, Kent, with George still in the cockpit.

David Buchanan, the then chairman of the group, had been told during 1971 that according to reliable local gossip a Hurricane had gone down in a swamp near Goudhurst and been abandoned. Intrigued, David set out to investigate. Initially, the clues were few and far between – sparse, to say the least. However, he eventually found a former ARP warden who had witnessed the crash at Bockingfold Farm and who willingly showed him where he said it had crashed. Of the pilot, nobody seemed sure what had happened although those who were there had seen no parachute. Of itself that was not necessarily indicative of the pilot's fate. He could well have baled out at high altitude, unseen by watchers on the ground, and drifted down to land safely many miles away. On the other hand, if he had gone down with his Hurricane then nobody locally had any recall of his body being found. The aeroplane itself had simply plunged into a swampy patch of ground in a small wooded strip just alongside a little stream and vanished.

Its location, tucked away in a secluded valley, was as remote as you could get in this part of the Weald of Kent. Not many visitors passed this way except for sheep and itinerant hop-pickers. That was as true for 1940 as it was for the 1970s and finding anyone who could corroborate the ARP man's story seemed an impossible task. For Dave Buchanan and his team that corroboration was important because they were single-mindedly intent on finding the wreckage. The only problem was that they couldn't find any trace of it based upon the witness's idea of its position.

However, the ex-warden was emphatic and David went back to the spot time and again to search. Each time he was met by failure. After one more search David was about to give up for good when a woman passed by, out walking her dog. Curious, she enquired what David was searching for. Her reply was a breath of fresh air in a search that had foundered. "You are in the wrong place," she told him! The lady in question lived nearby at Swan Cottage, Goudhurst, had seen the crash and said she knew for certain where it was. Searching the newly indicated spot David at once found pieces of aircraft wreckage easily identifiable as being from a Hurricane. The quest was back on.

As was the situation with the Gruszka case (see Chapter Six), work on finding and recovering wartime aircraft wrecks during the very late 1960s and early 70s was based largely on local information. This was mainly in the form of stories from eye witnesses of such events and very little else besides. As we have seen in the case of the ARP warden who recalled the Bockingfold crash, the reliability of witness recall was hugely variable. Sometimes, witnesses could no longer remember the exact spot where aeroplanes had fallen. Other times they were unfailingly correct. Equally, recall as to dates, times, aircraft types (or even nationality!) was fallible. There could be little or no reliance upon published sources for information because there virtually wasn't any – and official sources, both locally and nationally, were then very limited in the extreme in respect of availability. It really was a case, in those days, of building up a picture as to who, what and when. As one who was involved during those early pioneering days of aviation archaeology has put it, it was a case of "…the blind leading the partially sighted". Such was the case with the Bockingfold Farm crash. Until it was dug out of the ground the mystery behind it and its pilot would surely endure. Even then there would be no telling as to whether the story would unfold, or whether any recovered wreckage might just hold onto its secret. It was a hit and miss affair with no certainty as to outcomes.

In May 1972 Dave Buchanan and his team moved things forward and set up a major excavation of the Bockingfold Farm crash over the weekend of 21/22 May, bringing a mechanical excavator and water pump onto site. *(This, of course, pre-dated the requirement to seek authority for recovery from the MOD or to notify them of any intentions as to recovery.)* From the black mire of the Goudhurst swamp emerged masses of wreckage, including the Rolls-Royce Merlin engine and cockpit. The control column, retrieved from several feet of mud, still had its gun firing button set to FIRE.

Hurricane P2728 was the aircraft in which George Drake was lost. It is photographed here at a RAF maintenance unit before delivery to 607 Squadron when the code letters AF-C were applied.

Amongst the shattered cockpit lay the fragmented skeletal remains of its pilot, surrounded by remnants of his clothing and scattered personal effects. Amongst the sad personal items was a sewing kit, a cigarette case and a lucky charm from Clovelly. As soon as remains were first uncovered, David Buchanan and his team suspended work and contacted the police at Cranbrook. Nonplussed by this extraordinary event, the village policeman called in the coroner and the Commonwealth War Graves Commission who between them oversaw the continuance of the work and the careful removal of any further finds. In the run-up to the Remembrance weekend of 1972 the coroner for South Kent, Mr John Clarke, held an inquest on 7 November into the remains discovered at Bockingfold Farm and from evidence provided by the Ministry of Defence he was able to name the pilot as a twenty-year-old South African, Pilot Officer George James Drake of 607 Squadron, RAF Tangmere.

He had lost his life in an air battle over the Mayfield area on 9 September 1940

David Buchanan (centre) who led the team from the Ashford & Tenterden Aircraft Recovery Group shows George's brothers, Eric (left) and Arthur, the control column and Rolls-Royce Merlin engine from P2728 at the Brenzett Aeronautical Museum.

The recovery of George Drake's Hurricane underway at Bockingfold Farm, Goudhurst, during May 1972. The discovery of George Drake in the wreckage was the first post-war discovery of its kind in the United Kingdom.

and evidence of identification was made possible through the discovery of the aircraft serial number, P2728, found stencilled on parts of the wreckage. The serial number had provided a direct link to George Drake its pilot who had been posted as missing in action since 9 September 1940. The operations record book for 607 Squadron filled in some of the detail:

"Combat took place in the Mayfield area at about 17.30 hours. When the squadron was at 17,000ft some 60-70 enemy aircraft, possibly Ju 88s and Do 17s, were seen flying north in several formations of five. Squadron turned towards formation of bombers when escorting fighters, about 40-50 Me 109s, were seen to both sides and astern of the bombers at about 19,000ft. Blue section attacked the bombers from underneath with Green section doing rearguard action. With the bombers now too far ahead Sqn Ldr Vick ordered Red and Yellow sections to attack the fighters.

Our losses: Plt Off Parnall, Plt Off Lenahan & Plt Off Drake missing.

Sgt Burnell-Phillips, Sgt Spyer slightly wounded.

One Hurricane Cat 3

Three Hurricanes missing

Two Hurricanes Crashed

Enemy Losses: One Dornier 17 destroyed."

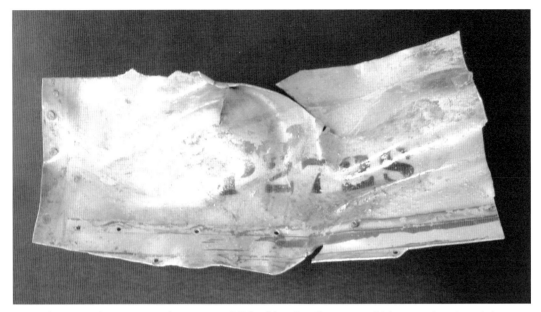

Identification of George Drake was established by the discovery of his aeroplane's serial number P2728 painted on various parts of the wreckage including this section of engine cowling panel.

It was the first occasion in which 607 Squadron had really tangled with the enemy during the Battle of Britain and George Drake had been flying in Yellow Section (Yellow 3) which had taken on the fighters. Of the twelve aircraft that had taken on the enemy formation six had actually been shot down, although the 607 Squadron operations record book fails to make mention of the sixth, Sgt J Landsdell, who was slightly wounded. It had been a rather shocking baptism of fire. One of the survivors of the slaughter was George Welford:

This broken fountain pen was found in the cockpit of George Drake's Hurricane. No doubt he used it to write his last combat report, make the last entry in his log book and to send his last letter home. A poignant and tragic little relic.

"We were well and truly bounced by Me109s on that day; we lost six out of twelve aircraft. Amongst them were my best friends Stuart Parnall and Scotty Lenahan. As no more was heard of George Drake his death was presumed. We were shocked. We just could not take it all in. Bloody good blokes, all of them."

Of the casualties, the bodies of George Welford's friends, Parnall and Lenahan, were both recovered from crash sites at Goudhurst and Cranbrook respectively, but of Drake no trace was ever found until the 1972 discovery. Although Dave Buchanan was later of the view that MOD records may well have indicated the location of the crash, any publicly available evidence pointing to Bockingfold Farm, which may have established any link to George Drake, was certainly limited. Indeed, the records of 49 Maintenance Unit who dealt with crashes in the region had also been somewhat vague. Often, these tabulated reports stated the aircraft serial number, location and date the wreck was cleared – thus providing a good basis on which to assemble a framework history for many of the losses recorded there. In the case of what must certainly refer to the Bockingfold Farm crash there is simply a single line entry. It reads:

"10 September 1940. Hurricane. Goudhurst. Not salved"

So, no clues there that might in any way link to the loss of George Drake save for the extremely tenuous pointers of aircraft type, the date the wreck was inspected and its general location. In the end it was only the recovery that unlocked the mystery but as with all these cases it also unlocked a good deal more besides.

In far-away South Africa the *Johannesburg Star* newspaper announced the discovery of one of its native war heroes and the story was immediately seen by George's stunned brothers, Eric and Arthur. Both brothers

Further evidence came to light with the discovery of the RAF Aeroplane Maintenance Form (the Form 700) which was found folded and stowed inside the map box. The still legible document confirmed the Hurricane to have been P2728 and established the individual aircraft code letter to be C.

travelled from South Africa to attend George's funeral, their tickets paid for by the *Johannesburg Star* and South African Airways. The funeral was movingly conducted by the RAF with full military honours at Brookwood Military Cemetery on 22 November 1972. The two brothers also travelled to Kent and viewed the wreckage of George's aeroplane in the Brenzett Aeronautical Museum on Romney Marsh and presented the museum with other personal artefacts relating to their late brother. They were also able to recall that George's cigarette case, found in the wreckage, had been won by him as a fairground prize. It was just one of those sad little human tales that so very often emerge with these stories.

Their joint gratitude for the ability to lay their brother to rest was more than tangible. Incredibly, it was only the discovery of George's body and the issue of a death certificate that enabled the final settlement of their late mother's will. The estate had been bequeathed in equal shares to the three brothers, but George's share had been left 'in limbo' pending confirmation of his death. All the time that his death was unconfirmed it had been the wish of their mother that George's share should remain frozen and held in trust in the event that he should one day turn up. Undoubtedly this was a tragic case of a grieving mother holding onto an illogical hope, against all sensibly realistic conclusions, that somehow and somewhere her son was still alive. In the absence of any evidence that George was dead, his mother refused to accept the finality of the situation.

It is not an uncommon phenomenon often encountered when loved ones simply go missing – even when persons go missing in wartime and all evidence points to their certain death. The twenty-first century expression might be "closure" and it is something that George Drake's mother never had. Rather cruelly perhaps, the tailors Messrs Gieves of London wrote to the Drake family in 1942 to say that a bill of £11 three shillings and threepence was outstanding for his RAF uniform and would they please settle at once? It somehow extended hope to George's mother. It was just that he was temporarily unavailable to pay and she would settle up for him in the meantime. Closure, though, was something that David Buchanan was eventually able to give to Eric and to Arthur Drake and it underlines the enduring value of putting such issues to rest – both in a literal and a metaphoric sense.

George James Drake, a long way from his South African home, had taken off from Tangmere during the height of the Battle of Britain and simply flown off into the blue never to be seen again. That is, not until the work of amateur enthusiasts and historians had unearthed the truth behind his disappearance. Commenting later on the discovery, the Ministry of Defence took the view that this was a one-off and that no other missing pilots were ever likely to be found in the UK. In fact, George Drake was the first of several who would eventually be discovered.

After their recovery of Pilot Officer George Drake, the Brenzett Aeronautical Museum mounted this display of paperwork and photographs relating to him – a good example of the work carried out by some museums in remembering and honouring the fallen.

CHAPTER 3

The Sad Secret of Daniels Wood

EDDIE EGAN'S mother and his sister Grace were far away from the scene of battle on the afternoon of 17 September 1940. Both were attending a film matinee in Scotland, but at around 3.40 Grace's mother went deathly pale and gazed at a clock on the wall. "He's dead. We'll never see him again," she said softly as she grasped Grace's hand. Within twenty-four hours the dreaded telegram arrived to confirm Mrs Egan's premonition. She had been expecting it ever since the blood had run icy cold through her veins that previous afternoon. Follow-up letters from Sqn Ldr Hogan, the commanding officer, and later from the Air Ministry offered merely platitudes suggesting that he was missing and not yet presumed dead. He might yet turn up somewhere, injured, or as a prisoner of war. The suggestions, intended to offer some consoling hope,

Sgt Pilot Edward James Egan was just nineteen years old when he vanished during a patrol with 501 Squadron on 17 September 1940. Here, he poses alongside a Hurricane of 615 Squadron with whom he served before a posting to 501 Squadron.

were futile. She absolutely knew that her nineteen-year-old Eddie had been killed. A mother's intuition told her all she needed to know and also told her what the Air Ministry could not yet confirm. He was dead. Sgt Pilot Tony Pickering, Eddie's great pal on 501 Squadron, also knew that Eddie was dead.

That afternoon twelve Hurricanes of 501 Squadron and eight of 253 Squadron had been ordered off from Kenley to patrol Tenterden at 17,000ft. In the formation, led by Sqn Ldr Hogan, were Sgts Lacey, Pickering and Egan. The formation had climbed up through broken cloud at six to eight thousand feet and found itself in clear sky above Tenterden moving northwards over Ashford and still climbing. By 15.35hrs they were circling at 18,000ft when a panic-stricken call crackled in the pilot's headphones: "Break! For Christ's sake break!"

Too late, Me109s had been spotted coming down in a diving attack and had torn through the now scattering and diving formation. Tony Pickering was still diving and turning – diving and turning to shake off potential attackers. Very soon Pickering had gone through the cloud and was down to 5,000ft, apparently all alone and somewhere in the Maidstone area. Suddenly, another aircraft was alongside. Pickering at once recognised it as Egan when he could read the Z-Zebra call sign on the fuselage side and the two chums flew alongside each other. Egan gave Pickering the thumbs-up and the two pilots grinned across the sky at each other as they flew on searching for the rest of the squadron. Rallying the troops, Hogan called the squadron to reform at Angels 13 over Maidstone and Egan and Pickering set off on a north-westerly course to find them. Emerging through the cloud, Pickering glimpsed what he took to be three Spitfires above and behind them.

Too late, he saw the black crosses as they came down on the two sergeant pilots. Almost as if he was watching something in slow motion, he saw the cannon shells and bullets rip into Egan's Z-Zebra. Peeling away and climbing to meet the attack, Pickering glimpsed Egan's bullet-riddled Hurricane falling away on fire. As it passed through the clouds beneath him they glowed crimson from the fire. Seconds later there was a momentary flash in a wood far below. There was no parachute.

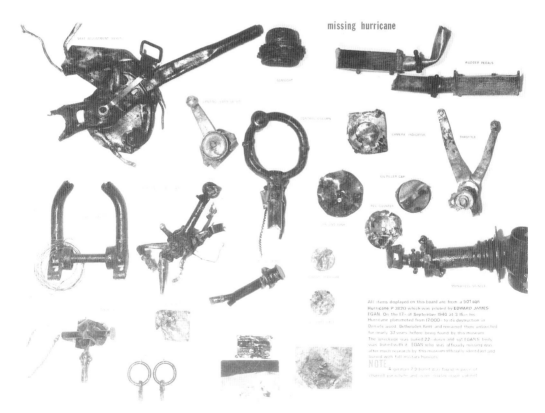

These few rather sad relics were virtually all that remained of Sgt Egan's Hurricane, P3820, when the wreckage was salvaged by the London Air Museum in 1976. The items include both rudder pedals, the control column, gun sight, cockpit controls and the tail wheel yoke. Eddie's mortal remains were also found in the wreck.

When he returned to Kenley, a shaken Pickering got out his flying maps and could pinpoint almost exactly the woods where Eddie's Hurricane had smashed into the ground. He told Hogan and he told the squadron intelligence officer during his post-combat debrief. Although Eddie was clearly dead, Pickering reasoned that somebody would surely find him. They didn't. Indeed, several months later Pickering was asked again to pinpoint the spot on a map. He heard no more about Eddie Egan until 1976.

It was in the summer of that year that Tony Graves and John Tickner had been told about a Hurricane crash site in Daniels Wood at Tuesnoad, Bethersden. It was a site that sounded both interesting and promising from an archaeological point of view and since the identity of the aeroplane

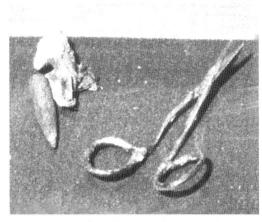

A small pair of nail scissors found in the wreckage were recognised by Eddie's sister as a gift she had given him. They helped convince the coroner as to the identity of the pilot. Also shown here is a fired German 7.92mm bullet embedded in a charred portion of parachute material. These sad little relics tell their own story.

was a bit of a mystery the challenge of recovering it to uncover its secrets was irresistible. So irresistible that on 11 September the pair organised its recovery by mechanical excavator. From almost fifteen feet of heavy clay emerged the badly smashed and burned wreckage and a few shattered portions of bone. Charred parachute material, parachute buckles and a bent pair of nail scissors told their own grim story. It was a tale that was far from over, though. Like many cases involving missing airmen from the Battle of Britain, it would yet have its own moments of high drama.

Calling an inquest, HM Coroner Dr Mary McHugh convened the hearing at Croydon on 25 February 1977 and took evidence from the recovery team, the police, a pathologist, Tony Pickering, the MOD and Eddie Egan's sister, Grace Summerville. Congratulating the team, the coroner pronounced that she was satisfied the remains were indeed those of Sgt Edward Egan who had lost his life due to enemy action on 17 September 1940. The Ministry of Defence, though, were not so sure and in a surprising move they unilaterally overturned the coroner's ruling. In the absence of any firm evidence that physically identified either the pilot personally, or his aircraft by its serial number, the MOD would not permit his burial as Sgt Edward Egan.

It was a shattering and utterly devastating blow to Grace Summerville who had said after the inquest that she had taken great comfort from knowing her brother had died in an ancient English wood and not on foreign soil. Now, after learning what had become of her brother, the MOD had pulled the rug from under her and would not permit the remains to be buried as Eddie, refusing to authorise the CWGC to erect a headstone bearing his name. In the eyes of the MOD Sgt Egan was still missing and on 9 March 1978, well over a year after the inquest, a military funeral was held at Brookwood Cemetery. Present at the ceremony was Eddie's sister Grace Summerville, friends and other relatives of Eddie Egan and former squadron colleague Tony Pickering. It was a slightly surreal event to say the very least. A funeral for an unknown airman attended by friends and relatives of Sgt Egan at a service where his name could not be mentioned and where the brass plate to the coffin read: "An Unknown Aviator Of The Second World War". It was a wholly unsatisfactory state of affairs.

To those involved in the recovery, and to other recovery organisations and individual researchers, the outcome was totally unacceptable. So unacceptable was it that something had to be done, and in a spirit of co-operation a team was assembled to re-excavate the site to search for any clues that might have been missed. It was a long-shot but one worth taking. There was nothing to lose. During November 1978 the original team members met up with others from the Brenzett Aeronautical Museum, the Kent Battle of Britain Museum and the Wealden Aviation Archaeological Group.

Together with a handful of other enthusiasts, the site was again carefully excavated although it soon became apparent that very little had been missed by Tony Graves or John Tickner the first time around. Just a few shards of alloy, some bits of charred wood and a single contorted engine valve was about all that turned up. The team was despondent but just as the excavation was about to be closed down it was Steve Hall of the Wealden group who broke open a large clod of clay and out fell a small rectangle of brass. Incredibly it was the Hurricane's main constructor's plate stamped with the serial number of Sgt Egan's aircraft – P3820. The missing link had been found and very shortly celebratory glasses were being raised by the whole team in a toast to young Eddie Egan in a nearby Headcorn pub! The amateurs had been vindicated. More importantly, the MOD were obligated to relent their previous position and instruct the CWGC to replace the headstone with one bearing the name of Sgt Edward Egan.

The missing link. This is the brass constructor's plate from Eddie Egan's Hurricane, found at Daniels Wood on 4 November 1978. It confirms the serial number to be P3820 which is shown in the bottom left hand box. This small item, no bigger than a matchbox, enabled the eventual identification of Sgt E J Egan to be made.

Exactly why Eddie Egan had remained missing for so long is a mystery that endures. Certainly Tony Pickering had had a pretty good idea where his friend had fallen, and local reports on the crash had pinpointed it accurately as well. Just why it was left and no attempt made to salvage it is a puzzle, especially as recovery would have been relatively uncomplicated at this site in 1940. Perhaps a clue, however, lies in the reports of the RAF's 49 Maintenance Unit. On a long list of aircraft crashes due for salvage there is an entry under 22 September which simply reads: "Hurricane – Bethersden – in hand." Most of the other aircraft on these lists carry the serial number of the machine involved. Not so the Bethersden crash. This could be explained, perhaps, by the fact that Sgt Egan's aircraft was so smashed and burned that no serial number was discernible to the crash inspector.

On the other hand, just a matter of yards from the Daniels Wood crash site another Hurricane had bellied-in with battle damage during the same combat, Plt Off Welford of 607 Squadron escaping with slight wounds from Hurricane P3929 at Tuesnoad Farm. Hurricane P3929 does not appear on that same 49 MU list as one might expect it to, and it would be fair to speculate that possibly the recovery crews sent to recover the un-numbered Hurricane (eg Sgt Egan's) had found George Welford's P3929 and salvaged that instead but left Egan's wreck behind. Either way, the fate of Sgt Egan was finally solved more than thirty-eight years later.

Originally buried in 1978 at Brookwood Military Cemetery in Surrey as an unknown RAF airman, the headstone was subsequently replaced when evidence of his Hurricane's serial number (P3820) later emerged. The inscription at its foot was chosen by Eddie's family and reads: "In Treasured Memory of a Much Loved One of The Few".

Those passing through the area today that is known as Daniels Water, and around Tuesnoad Farm, would also pass a field that had once been Daniels Wood. The wood that once held such a sad secret has been swept away in the interests of agricultural efficiency and those who locally recall the crash have now all gone. Only the data plate survives as a tangible reminder of the epic struggle to find and name this missing Battle of Britain pilot. When Tony Graves retired to France he took the mounted and framed brass plate with him, although in 2009 the identity plate came up for sale and was sold at Dreweatts Sale Rooms by auction. It can only be hoped that the new owner or any future owner of this trophy will always understand and appreciate its significance in enabling Edward Egan to be brought home.

> NOTE: The re-excavation of this particular crash site after the earlier retrieval of the pilot's remains had enabled Sgt Egan to be positively identified. In the case of Sgt Adair (see Chapter One) any such subsequent re-examination of the site that might yet establish the identity of the aircraft or pilot would be of somewhat limited value. Whilst it might establish conclusively that this was where Sgt Adair had died there exists no grave (as in the Egan case) where a headstone might be re-engraved with his name since HM Coroner in that case ordered the disposal of the remains found.

Missing to Friendly Fire?

T HE MORNING of 14 September 1940 dawned fine and bright and saw the Hurricane pilots of 73 Squadron called to readiness at RAF Castle Camps from dawn until 13.00hrs when they were eventually stood down for lunch. The nervous tension that had built all morning had not been broken. Called back to readiness at 15.30hrs the order came to scramble and proceed to North Weald at Angels 15 in company with 17 Squadron. Standing by dispersal Leading Aircraftsman Ken Rumbold raced to the nearest Hurricane and vaulted onto the wing, just in time to help Sgt John Brimble into the cockpit to secure his parachute and seat harness. As the engine roared into life blowing a slipstream of hot exhaust gasses across the still open cockpit, any conversation became impossible.

Rumbold caught Brimble's eye as the young pilot grinned and gave the thumbs-up. Slapping Brimble on the shoulder in a gesture of 'good-luck and mind how you go' Rumbold jumped to the ground and ducked out of the way as the tailplane of the already rolling Hurricane trundled past. Turning to watch, Rumbold screwed up his eyes against the bright sun and a warm blast of dust and grass cuttings while he saw 'his' Hurricane off. It was the last that anyone would see or hear of Sgt Brimble for exactly forty years.

Sgt John Joseph Brimble was shot down and killed in a Hurricane of 73 Squadron on 14 September 1940. He was posted as missing, believed killed. In fact, he had been found at the time of the crash and buried as an unknown RAF airman in Maidstone.

As with all actions of the period, the exploits of 73 Squadron as they went into battle that day were faithfully recorded in the operations record book which noted that only six Hurricanes returned following the afternoon scramble. Those that came back did so singly – the depleted numbers and the straggling nature of the return told its own story. The squadron had been split up and had taken a battering.

The first back was Fg Off Smith. Shaken, he reported that he had seen a Hurricane shot down by a Spitfire south of Tilbury and as Green Section (Sgts Plenderleith, Garton and Webster) followed Smith back, they too told the tale of the attack by a section of Spitfires that had broken up their formation at 16,000ft. Fg Off Scott and Plt Off Marchand were the only other two pilots to return – the latter having bullet holes in his port main tank, the port aileron, the main spar and another directly through the top of his radio mast. Of the others who did not return, news slowly filtered through and the adjutant's telephone took a steady stream of calls; Flt Lt Mike Beytagh was at West Malling and Sgt Marshall was safe with Kent Police. Sgt Leng called in from RAF Gravesend whilst hospitals telephoned with news of Sgt Griffin and the CO, Sqn Ldr Robinson. Neither was too badly hurt – at least, not life threateningly so. Of Sgt John Brimble there was no news, but on the ground sixteen-year-old George Underdown had watched as a Hurricane tumbled out of the battle above.

Coming straight down, the Hurricane seemed clearly doomed but then, as if the pilot had somehow recovered, it momentarily pulled up, faltered, and finally dived at full throttle into a meadow at Parkhouse Farm, Chart Sutton. By now such events were becoming increasingly commonplace but young George was curious that the sky above him seemed only to buzz with Spitfires and Hurricanes. Down in the meadow, smoke drifted away on the breeze from a crater gouged into the ground. Soldiers and police kept eager sightseers away as they picked some pitiful remains of the pilot from the jumble of wreckage and, eventually, filled in the shallow hole leaving nothing more to see.

Back at the airfield, the remnants of 73 Squadron were angered by the fate that had befallen them at the hands of 'friendly' Spitfires and the squadron intelligence officer, after he had gathered his surviving pilot's reports, typed an urgent signal to HQ Fighter Command calling for "…a further report on the matter". What, if anything, was any outcome of the intelligence officer's protestations is not clear from the following pages of the operations record book. The heat and tempo of battle was increasing and the very next day the squadron was to lose Pilot Officer Roy Marchand, shot down in flames and killed over Sittingbourne. Sgt A E Marshall, shot down in the 14 September debacle, must have wondered who the enemy was when he was again shot down on 17 September and had to make a forced-landing at Wick Farm, Burnham. This time his attacker had been a Hurricane! It is, though, the events of 14 September 1940 that concern us here.

As it approached north Kent and an anticipated encounter with enemy aircraft, 73 Squadron was still climbing and in line-astern. Suddenly, the attacking Spitfires were upon them and the squadron was spilt up and scattering across the sky. The result we now know, and although we have no knowledge of any investigation into the event by Fighter Command, it is possible to identity the attacking Spitfires as being from either 222 or 603 Squadron. 66 Squadron were also in the area and might also have been involved. The operations record books of 222 and 603 Squadrons, and the individual combat reports of some of the pilots involved, help to clarify what went on. 'Clarify', however, is a somewhat subjective assessment of any form of insight these reports actually give us. Suffice to say, though, that the combat report for one of 222's pilots attracts some attention.

"I was with the squadron when we went into attack a group of Me 109s. I selected one as my target and opened fire at 250 yards, closing to about 100 yards, during which I fired three bursts of approximately three seconds each. Some parts of the machine fell past me. He went into a dive which got steeper as he went down and I followed him, giving him two very short bursts at 250 yards range. He went straight through a cloud and when I came out below it I could see him still diving for the ground. I understand from the Detling Controller that he pulled out a very little and then dived straight in. On the same flight but in another combat my machine was damaged and I was forced to land at Detling."

The timing and place of the attack make it difficult to apportion any specific Luftwaffe loss to this claim. In fact, there are none that fit. Away to the north east, near Teynham, one Me109 was shot down (probably by 253 Squadron) and exploded at around 16.00 hours – but its location some ten miles from Detling makes it an impossibility that it might have been seen from Detling. High up on the Downs, RAF Detling overlooks the Kentish Weald and gazes straight down on Chart Sutton some three or so miles to the south. Personnel on the aerodrome might well have seen a diving fighter, but at this distance it would have almost certainly been impossible to tell whether British or German.

There is also the uncanny description from Detling of the claimed victim diving, pulling out slightly and then diving in. The account mirrors closely what George Underdown said that he saw from his vantage point close to Sgt Brimble's crash. Either way, this is not in any way to apportion 'blame'. This author has already explored in another work (*Bader's Last Fight*: Grub Street) the matter of so-called friendly fire. That it was a not-infrequent occurrence in combat situations like this is a matter of fact, and in the case of 73 Squadron's experience on 14 September 1940 the record held at The National Archives is absolutely clear. They were attacked by Spitfires. Taking the issue to a further conclusion, the only Spitfires in the area who might be considered were those of 66, 222 and 603 Squadrons.

Of further interest is the report from 603 Squadron that the Me 109s they saw were in line-astern. It might just be coincidence, but we know that 73 Squadron were in line-astern when they approached the battle zone. As for 603 Squadron, Fg Off Boulter sent one Me 109 crashing earthwards, watching as it rolled onto its back and diving into the ground where it then caught fire. Again, there is some difficulty in attributing a loss to this claim although no such difficulty arises with Fg Off B R Macnamara's victory. He shot down an Me 109 that then landed wheels up at Boxley Hill, near Maidstone. The pilot, Fw Ettler of 1/JG77, scrambled clear and set light to his Messerschmitt. Circling above, Macnamara sprayed the area with a few bursts of fire but he was ultimately unable to dissuade Ettler from torching his aeroplane. The sorry affair that saw 73 Squadron take such a battering from their own side was just another small episode in the bigger picture that was the Battle of Britain.

Picking up the pieces of a story about a crashed Hurricane at Chart Sutton in 1979, Steve Vizard had managed to persuade the landowner to allow him to excavate the following year

John Brimble enjoys a seaside picnic with a colleague during his initial training as a pilot although he has not yet been awarded his pilot's wings. John holds his cigarette case which would turn up again forty years later.

and with a sense of history Steve elected to dig there on 14 September 1980. Already it seemed likely from local reports that the crash had taken place exactly forty years earlier, but George Underdown was as certain as he could be that the pilot had not escaped although he had remembered remains being retrieved from the crash crater.

If it were the case that the pilot had been killed then really only one candidate fitted the frame for that day: Sgt Brimble. The problem was, of course, that Sgt Brimble was technically still missing. In this context, the word *technically* is used advisedly because one of two burials at the Bell Road (Milton) Cemetery in Sittingbourne on 28 September 1940 (see also Chapter Fourteen, Known Unto God) of unknown airmen was of the unidentified remains of an RAF pilot who died at Parkhouse Farm, Chart Sutton, on 14 September 1940. Buried in plot W.49 the remains were clearly those George Underdown had remembered being recovered. So, if the pilot at Parkhouse Farm, Chart Sutton, was indeed John Brimble then it seemed clear that he had already been buried – but as an unknown pilot.

Excavations at the site on the exact fortieth anniversary of the crash quickly uncovered wreckage just below the plough line and in which was revealed a parachute, personal effects and human remains. Amongst the torn paperwork was a cheque book bearing the name of John Joseph Brimble along with an identity disc. Proof positive was given the extra confirmation by the discovery of the aeroplane serial number, P2542. It had been recorded

as the Hurricane in which Sgt Brimble had been lost on 14 September 1940. Here was a case of a pilot's *partial* remains being recovered in 1940 and not identified.

Press interest in the case was intense, with accusations of the dig being callous and uncaring. It was, perhaps, rather unfair criticism given that the finds at Chart Sutton should have allowed plot W.49 to have a new stone erected with Sgt Brimble's name inscribed. The further remains from Parkhouse Farm ought properly to have been simply interred at Sittingbourne, the status of Brimble as a missing casualty amended and any surviving

That same cigarette case, rather crumpled, was discovered in the wreckage of John Brimble's Hurricane at Chart Sutton in Kent on the exact fortieth anniversary of his loss – 14 September 1980. With it was a folded one pound note.

family duly notified. It was, after all, not surprising that whatever had been buried in 1940 had not been identified. As events in 1980 had shown, the means by which to identify that pilot had never been found.

However, it is indeed surprising that the MOD made absolutely no link between the 1980 finds and the burial at Sittingbourne when the evidence already and very clearly existed, both in the form of a death certificate and the Sittingbourne burial register, that this pilot had certainly already been buried! Instead, the MOD pressed ahead with plans for another funeral with full military honours which was attended by John's elder brother, Bill, at Brookwood on 16 October 1980. Standing quietly in a grove of fir trees adjacent to the grave site, an elderly veteran doffed his cap and bit his bottom lip while a volley of rifle fire rang out in salute. Ken Rumbold had travelled to pay his last respects. "I saw him off in 1940," he said. "It's only right I see the poor chap off now."

When the silence returned to Brookwood Cemetery after the bugle calls and rifle fire, it did not quieten the press interest nor the controversy. Readers' letters to local newspapers were filled with those who were supportive and those who were not. The *Daily Telegraph*, too, took up the issue and even managed to bring Sir Douglas Bader into the fray. Quoting Bader, the newspaper reported his comments:

"It is a very personal thing. If it were my brother or father I would like to know. There are many people who lost relatives in combat and who were never found and I think they would like to know what happened to them so that they can have a Christian burial."

Support for Bader's opinion, according to that same newspaper, also came from Wing Commander Bob Stanford Tuck who subscribed to the view that members of The Few should not be left in tangled aluminium graves. The *Kent Messenger*, too, carried support for the recovery of Sgt Brimble in its editorial comment column:

"Controversy has raged in *The Kent Messenger* for some weeks about whether it was right for an aircraft recovery group to dig up a wartime fighter and the remains of its pilot.

"It has been suggested that to do so brings back unhappy memories for bereaved families, but more forcefully we believe it has been argued that the courage of those who protected our country should be marked with more than sheep droppings in a distant field.

"Most of those from whom we have heard have been gratified to know what happened to their sons and brothers and have been pleased that a proper resting place has been granted them.

"The recovery of planes and pilots should be monitored carefully to ensure that it is done decently, as it was recently at Chart Sutton."

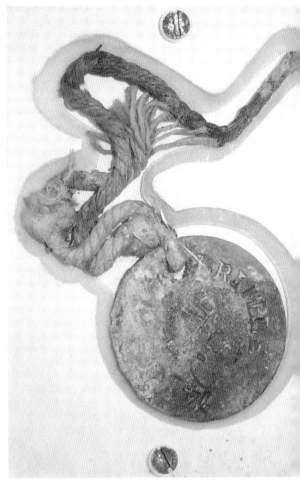

Had this identity disc been found in 1940 it would have saved forty years of anguish and of not knowing for the Brimble family. Picked up at the crash site long after the event, and clearly marked with Sgt Brimble's name and service number, it is now displayed at the Shoreham Aircraft Museum in Kent as a tribute to the young pilot.

On the other hand, of course, the MOD continued to be vehemently opposed to recoveries such as this. Perhaps badly stung by criticism for their inertia in dealing with casualties like Brimble, and on the back of three such recoveries inside a year (Hubert Adair, Hugh Beresford and now John Brimble) the MOD stance through the press was overtly aggressive and stated that they were demanding an explanation from the recovery team for their actions. On the other hand, no explanation was ever forthcoming from the MOD for its failure to connect Sgt Brimble with the unknown airman already buried at Sittingbourne. It was a shameful oversight or failure. The MOD did concede, though, that some conflict and confrontation now existed between the amateur historians and themselves. Commenting to *The Kent Advertiser* on 30 September 1980, an MOD spokesperson said that:

"As a result of recent events there is a certain amount of distrust on both sides."

Despite all of this, John Brimble was no longer missing. His family remained very private in how they dealt with the matter but it is known that John's mother had died not long before the circumstances of his disappearance had finally been solved. She was 101. Evidently she had doted on John, and had longed to know what had become of him. What a great pity that she could not have had the comfort of finding the truth during her lifetime. The emergence of a situation where a grieving mother had died not knowing what had become of her son, or a case where a casualty ended up with more than one grave, was not to be unique in the catalogue of casualties dealt with in these chapters.

In ending our examination of the case of John Brimble we must turn again to the operations record book for 73 Squadron. On 13 September, the day prior to John's loss, the following is recorded:

"The station adjutant at Debden telephoned to say that he had had a message from Group that the body of Flt Lt Lovett was in the mortuary at Billericay and had been there for about four or five days and asking whether we had heard about it. It was our first intimation of 'Reggie' Lovett since he went out on patrol on the 7th and we are all disgusted to think that he has been lying un-coffined in the mortuary all this time. It would seem, from the scant information available, that someone has blundered badly."

In effect, this is Sgt Brimble's official grave. He was laid to rest here at Brookwood Military Cemetery as the Central Band of the Royal Air Force solemnly played Revd. C Harris's tune "The Supreme Sacrifice". Meanwhile, he also has a second grave as an unknown RAF airman at Bell Road Cemetery, Sittingbourne.

What irony that the 73 Squadron records should make these comments about someone blundering badly, and about a squadron member lying dead and unforgotten just the very day before Sgt Brimble vanished. What would the squadron diarist have to say, one wonders, had he still been recording events in 1980?

CHAPTER 5

Case Not Proven

METAL DETECTORISTS searching for Roman coins at Blackacre in Theydon Bois, Essex, during the mid-1970s stumbled accidentaly across the first clues that might have solved the mystery of Pilot Officer John Benzie. A Canadian Hurricane pilot with Sqn Ldr Douglas Bader's 242 Squadron, he had vanished somewhere in the London/Essex area during the heavy fighting of 7 September 1940. No trace of him had ever been found, but with recent national press attention spotlighting the activities of Tony Graves and John Tickner and their London Air Museum, it was not long before the coin hunters had contacted Tony and John to tell them what they had discovered. All the metal detecting enthusiasts could say was that they had found parts of aircraft wreckage. Nothing more.

However, John and Tony had previously heard about the site and had even resorted to using aerial infra-red photography in an

Pilot Officer John 'Jack' Benzie was a Canadian who served under Douglas Bader in 242 Squadron during the Battle of Britain. He disappeared when flying from RAF Coltishall during a combat over the east of London on 7 September 1940 and is still listed as missing.

attempt to identify the spot during what had been a search spanning five years. Visiting the site, the pair pinpointed the crash in the sloping field which runs just alongside the London Underground railway line at Blackacre. Tony and John quickly established that the aeroplane had been a Hurricane. It was clearly an interesting location, although absolutely nothing was known about it. Nonetheless, the pair secured permission to dig there and carried out an excavation during 1976. From a depth of eighteen feet emerged the Merlin engine and cockpit wreckage, and with it the skeletal remains of the pilot. Everything had been very badly burned and despite an extensive search nothing could be found that might identify

Benzie had also served with 242 Squadron during the Battle of France and was shot down on 23 May 1940 baling out of Hurricane P2550 south-west of Ypres. He is pictured here at around this period with his Hurricane LE-B at Biggin Hill. Jack Benzie flew aircraft coded B whenever he could as he regarded it as lucky – B for Benzie.

either the aircraft or pilot. Local information, too, was scant although some evidence seemed to point to a crash during the late afternoon of 7 September 1940. However, with the absence of literally any clues – save for the fact that this was a Hurricane pilot – the MOD really had no choice other than to declare that this man was an unknown airman. Consequently, he was buried at Brookwood Military Cemetery on 15 July 1977 in Plot 22, Row E, Grave No 1.

The decision not to name him was clearly the right one. After all, and even if it *could* be established that the crash had happened on 7 September 1940, there were three missing Hurricane pilots that day to consider; namely, Plt Off J Benzie of 242 Squadron, Flt Lt H R A Beresford and Fg Off L R G Mitchell of 257 Squadron. Although Beresford had crashed at Spit End Point, Elmley, on the Isle of Sheppey and was subsequently recovered and identified this was not until 1979 and so the Blackacre find pre-dated the discovery of Beresford by some three years. *(Unfortunately, some published sources have dated the Blackacre recovery as 1980 although this is certainly incorrect.)* So, with three possibilities to consider and with no evidence to go on the MOD had to take the 'unknown' route.

When the London Air Museum exhibited items from the site they did so by describing it as Hurricane P2962 – the aircraft in which Benzie had been lost. Of course, the museum already knew of the establishment of Beresford's crash location by the Kent Battle of Britain and it was reasonable to assume that Lancelot Mitchell, lost in the same action with Beresford, had probably been shot down close to Beresford. The conclusion that the

Theydon Bois crash had involved Benzie was not an unreasonable one. However, there was no confirming evidence to support the theory although the general location of the crash pretty much fitted in with Benzie's last known position. However, a museum collection had 'identified' the fate of a missing pilot. With the pilot now buried as 'unknown' it was decided in 1981 to re-excavate the site to search for fresh clues. There were none, but perhaps the clue was there already and had all along been included in the London Air Museum exhibit? Fixed to the display board the author spotted the torn-off corner of the data plate from the Rolls-Royce Merlin engine bearing the engine number 174050. Could it be matched to the records for Hurricane P2962?

The Royal Air Force Museum at Hendon holds the AM Form 78s for all wartime aircraft and these are, in effect, the aviation equivalent of a vehicular log book. For P2962 the engine number is recorded as 144702. No match. However, the fact that the engine number does not match the one found at Theydon Bois does not *exclude* the possibility that this was, after all, Jack Benzie's aeroplane and mortal remains. The reason, quite simply, is that these aircraft were often subject to engine changes during their service life and such changes were not always recorded on the AM Form 78.

The engine number recorded on the form was usually of the engine that aeroplane had

The name of

Pilot Officer John Benzie

was mentioned with proud thanksgiving,
in the prayers of

St. George's
Chapel of Remembrance

Royal Air Force Station,
Biggin Hill, Kent.

on the anniversary of his last
operational flight.

"All these were honoured in their generations, and were the glory of their times . . . . Their bodies are buried in peace, but their name liveth for evermore."

(*Ecclesiasticus* 44)

Although he had not flown from RAF Biggin Hill during the Battle of Britain, and his squadron was not operational there at all during that period, Jack Benzie was rather oddly remembered on the Roll of Honour at St George's Chapel of Remembrance RAF Biggin Hill as this commemorative scroll shows.

HURRICANE P·2962

CONTROL COLUMN

TURNING INDICATOR

K1 GAS PUMP

PITOT TUBE

TIMER

UNDERCARRIAGE CONTROL

DURING THE 1940s RAID ON THE ROYAL LONDON DOCKS ON THE 7TH SEPTEMBER 1940 DOUGLAS BADERS 242 SQN WAS SCRAMBLED FROM DUXDEN IN ESSEX A DOGFIGHT WITH JOHN 109 AND me109S ENSUED AND THIS HURRICANE FLOWN BY VZ BENZI A 25YEAR OLD CANADIAN WAS HIT AND DIVED VERTICALLY INTO THE GROUND IT TOOK FIVE WEEKS TO LOCATE THE SITE BY INFRA RED PHOTOGRAPHY AND p3 BENZI WHO WAS OFFICIALLY MISSING WAS FOUND WITH HIS AIRCRAFT AT A DEPTH OF 18FT AT THEYDON BOIS ESSEX

HARNESS BUCKLES

PICKETING RING

During 1976 the London Air Museum excavated wreckage from the crash site of a Hurricane at Blackacre, Theydon Bois, in Essex. The skeletal remains of the pilot were still in the cockpit. Unfortunately, the aircraft had burnt fiercely – probably before and after impact with the ground. All trace of identification had therefore been lost in the inferno. Although the museum team 'identified' the aircraft as P2962 in their display there was simply no evidence to corroborate this and the remains of the pilot were ultimately buried at Brookwood as an unknown RAF airman. The artefacts shown here bear a striking similarity to those uncovered during the Egan recovery, although in this case the best hope for any positive identification was the engine number on the plate displayed below the gun sight (top right).

been delivered with. So, a match with that number would have been conclusive but a non-match is simply unhelpful but does not rule out Benzie. Unfortunately, the truth about the identity of the Blackacre casualty may never be known although Jack Benzie has hardly gone un-commemorated. In his native Canada, the huge Lake Benzie was named after this young officer and on 7 September 1990, the fiftieth anniversary of his loss, parts of what may have been Plt Off Benzie's Hurricane were placed in the centre of Lake Benzie by the Royal Canadian Air Force in a symbolic gesture after they had been supplied, on request, to John Benzie's brother, James, by the author.

The case of a Hurricane pilot shot down over Essex two days before Benzie is another that has defied resolution – and yet, frustratingly, there is evidence to confirm the crash location. Jack Friedlein was working at his farm, Whitehouse Farm, in North Fambridge during the late afternoon of 5 September 1940 when a mighty explosion and ball of flame erupted without warning from near his chicken sheds. It had come so suddenly that he assumed it must have been a bomb dropped from a battle that had been raging above. He had seen or heard no approaching aircraft. Just a tremendous explosion. When he got to the spot there was just a hole in the ground and bits of tangled wreckage. Only then did it register that this had been an aeroplane. Other than that, he had little idea what had happened. The local authorities were equally vague, with a brief report entered by the Billericay Region Air Raid Warden's Log. For 5 September 1940 it simply recorded:

> "At 1530 hrs North Fambridge, near Post Office. Machine burnt out. British markings. Occupants – no trace. Plane buried ten to fifteen feet in ground. Pilot believed to be in wreckage."

This was the scene at Whitehouse Farm in North Fambridge, Essex, on 5 September 1940 after a Hurricane had crashed by Jack Friedlein's chicken sheds. Smoke drifts gently away on the breeze and scattered debris litters the field.

When the fire had died down Jack Friedlein was able to approach the crash site where he took this photo. The force of impact has left a shallow crater but driven the Hurricane and its pilot deep underground, leaving no more than tangled scraps that are unrecognisable as ever having been an aeroplane – let alone a Hurricane!

In the summer of 1979 the same chicken sheds were still there and provided a perfect reference point to locate the crash site which was then excavated by the London Air Museum team.

If the clues were vague in this report then they were, at least, sufficient to identify that the aircraft must have been a Hurricane and given that only one Hurricane pilot was missing that day, 5 September 1940, the aircraft had to be P3224 of 73 Squadron, flown by Glaswegian Sgt Alexander McNay. There were no other possibilities. In the summer of 1979 Tony Graves and John Tickner excavated the crash site and invited historian Peter Cornwell and the author to be present. From a depth of almost fifteen feet shattered remnants of a Hurricane emerged, including head armour, seat harness parts and the remains of an engine.

Of the pilot, there was simply no tangible evidence save for a portion of Mae West and a tattered RAF map bearing its original owner's name – the inscription McNAY clearly pencilled onto its buff cover. What had caused McNay's total disappearance in this way was a mystery. Had something been missed? Some years later the site came under further investigation by other enthusiasts intent on solving the riddle. Something had indeed been missed. A few shards of alloy turned up along with the more significant spade-grip of the control column. Again, of the pilot there was simply not any trace. The place that Sgt McNay had been lost had clearly been confirmed, but that was all. Alexander McNay, like John Benzie, remains missing.

If Sgt McNay had completely disappeared, and notwithstanding that his Hurricane had been found and identified, then he was not the only Battle of Britain pilot to have simply vanished without trace despite the discovery of associated aircraft

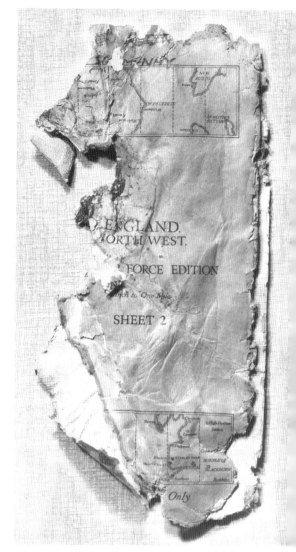

Despite a thorough excavation and an investigation of the recovered items not a trace of the pilot was found, although research had already established its pilot could only have been Sgt Alexander McNay of 73 Squadron. Indeed, amongst the recovered artefacts was this unburnt portion of a RAF flying map with the name Sgt McNay pencilled at its top. Aside from a portion of lifejacket no other sign of the pilot could be found in 1979.

wreckage. Another case in point is that of Polish pilot Sgt Stanislav Duszynski of 238 Squadron, shot down on 11 September 1940. That he had died when his aircraft crashed at Little Scotney near Lydd on Romney Marsh was established beyond any doubt by David Buchanan's Brenzett Aeronautical Museum team.

On 13 January 1973, the year after they had discovered Plt Off George Drake, the Brenzett group excavated the crash site at Little Scotney. They had no idea what they might find, and even less idea as to the identity of the aircraft type or its pilot. Not many feet below the marsh was their answer; Hurricane wreckage, a parachute and a black shoe. Amongst the wreckage, or what little of it remained, was the serial number R2682 which could be tied to the loss of Sgt Duszynski who was still missing. Of the pilot, nothing could be found before the excavation became unstable through flooding and collapsed.

David Buchanan's Brenzett team were clearly beyond reproach but, concerned about what they had found, they reported the matter to the Ministry of Defence casualty section. David had fully intended to go back on the site in better weather conditions and using more suitable machinery but, before he could do so, the Tenterden Police had contacted him to say that he was to take no further action in the matter. Instead, the work would be carried out by the RAF and on Tuesday 6 March 1973 David accompanied Fg Off D H Atton of 71 MU, RAF Bicester, to show him the precise crash location. After that, all

A subsequent re-excavation to search for missing clues was also mounted at the McNay crash site. Again, nothing tangible came to light other than the control column top with its gun button set to fire that had been missed in 1979. Although Sgt McNay had been holding this grip when shot down on 5 September 1940, no trace of this pilot has ever been found and at the time of writing this book he is still unaccounted for.

David knew was that the RAF had recovered whatever remained on site but he was hugely surprised to hear no reports of the discovery of the remains of Sgt Duszynski.

From what he knew and had previously found at the site he was as certain as he could be that they must have been there. If they were, then it remains a mystery as to what became of them. In 2008 the author tracked down the former RAF officer responsible, D H Atton. Mr Atton confirmed that he had been involved with that task and would check his diaries for further information. This would have certainly been helpful in resolving the case but ultimately Mr Atton declined to come forward with any information.

If all efforts by the Brenzett team and by the author to establish what had become of Sgt Duszynski had failed, investigator Mark Kirby was not going to let matters rest. Indeed, like many other researchers, he was puzzled by what the RAF had or had not found in 1973. He was determined to try to find out. In fact, his efforts were pre-dated shortly by the author who pressed the authorities to act and eventually accompanied the Polish consul-general in London, Dr Janusz Kochanowski, to the crash site with the local coroner's officer.

A quantity of bones were found scattered around the crash site and these were taken away by the police. Subsequently, the pathologist identified these as animal related. The author was unconvinced and asked Dr Susan MacLaughlin, a forensic osteologist, to survey the field. She did just that, and found three human bones – two metatarsals and one metacarpal. Here was evidence that Sgt Duszynski had died at this place, although, rather bizarrely, Dr MacLaughlin did cast doubts over how the bones had got there! Either way, the Poles placed pressure upon the MOD in December 1991 to re-excavate the site and this was agreed to. Then, without warning, came a further letter from the Polish consulate. It was dated 11 September 1992 (coincidentally the anniversary of the crash) and stated simply:

"Recently, the Consulate of the Republic of Poland has been advised by the family of Sgt Duszynski to abandon the further steps to search for the remains. I would like to express my sincere gratitude to you for your efforts and assistance in this matter."

This bleak setting in a field at Little Scotney on Romney Marsh, overlooked by a derelict farm cottage, is most likely the last resting place of Sgt Stanislav Duszynski of 238 Squadron, shot down here on 11 September 1940. Despite three excavations at this site by the Brenzett Aeronautical Museum, by the RAF and by Mark Kirby it seems that, like Sgt McNay, Stanislav Duszynski has simply vanished. Again, like Sgt McNay, evidence of identification clearly emerged – but of the pilot nothing was never found.

It was an astonishing turn-about, although when Mark Kirby took up matters again in 1986 he put in a telephone call to Duszynski's relatives in Torun, Poland. They apparently knew nothing of past events and declared no knowledge of any instruction to cease investigations. Indeed, they knew of no investigations! Further, they were extremely anxious that Mark should press ahead with a site investigation. The farmer, John Paine, was sympathetic to Mark's quest and wrote, commenting:

> "It is sad to think we have been cultivating over the remains for so many years without realising it."

Pre-dating Mark's interest in the case by some sixteen years the head of the RAF Air Historical Branch, Air Commodore Henry Probert, had written of the Duszynski case in October 1980. He commented:

> "The Hurricane which is thought to contain the Polish pilot's remains crashed into very soft ground and when attempts were made in 1973 to recover it – both by a private recovery group and by an official RAF recovery team – it was found impossible to excavate below twelve feet because of running sand. Since there was no means of telling just how much more work would need to be done, how long it would take, or how much it would cost, it was decided to go no further."

On 24 August 1996, Mark Kirby excavated the site again in an effort to solve the riddle. All he found in what was an enormous and comprehensive excavation (many feet deeper than the twelve feet mentioned by Air Cdr Probert) was to be a few kilos of insignificant aircraft debris. Of the pilot there was absolutely not a trace. The riddle remained. If anyone might be able to help solve it, then it might possibly be Mr Atton. But he has remained silent. The only clue was in Henry Probert's letter which seemed to indicate the RAF had abandoned the site in 1973 having met with no success. As to Mark's dig, it was again unlicensed and not for the first time did he find himself being arrested by Kent Police and charged with unlawfully carrying out a recovery without the appropriate legal authority.

His lawyer (who also happened to be John Tickner formerly of the London Air Museum) entered a robust defence of his client and pointed out that (a) very little of the aircraft had been found (b) no human remains were discovered and (c) that the site had already been subject to excavation and clearance by the RAF during March 1973. The prosecution was dropped and never went to court after the matter of the RAF's previous excavation had been raised as a defence issue. Meanwhile, the curious case of Sgt Stanislav Duszynski's disappearance endures.

Some mysteries, though, have been solved when all the initial evidence has pointed originally to a completely different aircraft type and pilot. Such was the case with Plt Off Colin Francis, a Hurricane pilot lost with 253 Squadron on 30 August 1940. Whilst not an accidental discovery, *per se*, the finds at Wrotham Hill, Kent, during 1981 were certainly a surprise for local enthusiast Bill Blundell. He had known about the crash of an aircraft at Percival's Farm, Wrotham Hill, for some time and had tried to track down details. The problem was, however, that nobody had ever heard of Percival's Farm and it wasn't shown on any maps.

It was a problem that solved itself, however, when Bill heard that somebody had been digging up aircraft wreckage at Wrotham Hill Farm. Going to the site Bill managed to find the farm manager who recalled that the former owner of the farm had been a Mr Percival. So, *this* was Percival's Farm and this *had* to be the 30 August 1940 crash site. Keen to find out more about the mystery aeroplane, Bill secured the farmer's permission to go digging although whoever had been digging there beforehand was unknown and their work clearly surreptitious and unauthorised. Without many clues to work on, however, Bill consulted aviation historians Alan Brown and Peter Cornwell who specialised in Battle of Britain losses. Both concurred that this was most likely the crash site of a Spitfire lost on 30 August 1940 when Fg Off J S Bell of 616 Squadron had been shot down near West Malling which is just a short distance from Wrotham Hill. Although Bell had been killed he was not missing.

Photographs of aircraft flown by the pilots detailed in this book have been hard to find, but a rather unusual image that emerged was this one which can be tied to Hurricane L1965 in which Pilot Officer Colin Francis of 253 Squadron was lost on 30 August 1940. Taken from an official series of Hawker photographs depicting the construction process of the Hurricane aircraft, this shot of the removable first aid panel is stencilled in black paint with the serial number L1965 – the aircraft in which Francis was lost. One of the factory workers, however, seems to have suffered a momentary lapse and has chalked '1695' in the corner!

From Bill's excavations at the site, it very soon became apparent that this was a Hurricane and he was joined in his physical endeavours to dig out the heavy clay by other like-minded enthusiasts. Before long, however, a parachute and uniform material had been unearthed and work was suspended whilst the advice of the MOD was sought. Having considered the matter, the MOD decided that the team had best continue operations under the supervision of a flight lieutenant, a fire-fighter and a medical orderly from nearby RAF Biggin Hill and in due course the wreckage and pilot were extricated from almost fourteen feet of clay. Evidence of identification was straightforward, the aircraft serial number L1965 being discovered in the cockpit linked directly to the loss of Plt Off Colin Dunstan Francis. Further confirmation was provided by a wrist watch with the name 'Colin' engraved on its back.

Little or no evidence existed prior to this excavation to suggest that the aeroplane was that which had been flown by Colin Francis and lost there on 30 August 1940. Many if not most of the cases dealt with here have had a 'provisional' identity established before recovery. It was not the case in respect of Colin Francis's Hurricane. Indeed, the loss had been previously thought by researchers to have been Fg Off Bell's 616 Squadron Spitfire, X4248. *(Interestingly, the crash location of X4248 has never been positively identified since the discovery of Colin Francis proved that it was not at Wrotham Hill.)*

The actions in which 253 Squadron had been engaged on 30 August had come the day after the squadron had been posted south to RAF Kenley from the quiet haven of Prestwick. Newly thrown into battle it had been a costly day for the squadron. By the day's end, 253 Squadron had lost three pilots killed or missing. In total, the squadron had lost five Hurricanes and had another pilot wounded. A further three Hurricanes had returned to base damaged. Leading Colin Francis's section had been Sqn Ldr Tom Gleave:

> "Sqn Ldr Gleave, leading the emergency section (Flt Lt Brown and Plt Off Francis) attacked the Me 109s which were trying to get on to the tails of our fighters. He saw one dive away with smoke pouring from the port wing and a second one turned on its side with the nose up and slid away out of sight, giving him the impression that the pilot had been knocked out. None of the other pilots observed any material results from their fire, though several saw bullets going into the enemy aircraft."

Francis did not return. The very next day, Tom Gleave was unfortunately shot down and horribly burned over Biggin Hill and the 253 Squadron commanding officer, Sqn Ldr H M Starr, was killed in action.

When Colin Francis was finally laid to rest at Brookwood on 29 September 1981, Group Captain Tom Gleave was in attendance to say farewell. Also there was George Brown, who had also been one of the 253 Squadron pilots shot down in the same dogfight. "He was a damned fine kid with lots of guts," commented Gleave at the funeral. He could well have been speaking about any of the pilots covered in this book.

CHAPTER 6

An Unforgotten Pole

Although a rather grainy photograph from the album of the late Squadron Leader Dave Glaser, this is Flying Officer Gruszka (right) with the other Pole on 65 Squadron, Pilot Officer Szulkowski, pictured at RAF Rochford just a day or so before Gruszka was lost. A squadron Spitfire waits at readiness beyond the garden hedge. Pilots at readiness and waiting to scramble lazed in the garden chair swing and raced for action through a gap in the hedge.

WHILST 15 September 1940 is celebrated as Battle of Britain Day, the hardest fought day of the entire battle in terms of losses on both sides was in fact 18 August. It was a day that saw dramatic and heavy raids against airfields and other targets in the south-east of England against which were pitched all of the squadrons at 11 Group's disposal. Amongst the ten RAF fighter pilots killed that day was a thirty-year-old Pole, Franciszek Gruszka, serving as a flying officer on Spitfires with 65 Squadron. As we will see, there is a degree of confusion as to the accurate timing of Gruszka's loss but according to the Ministry of Defence records contained within this officer's casualty file it was apparently indicated that: "Flying Officer Gruszka was last seen chasing enemy aircraft between Canterbury and Maidstone at about 14.50hrs on 18 August 1940." Until the

1970s that was the last that was ever seen of him and with no known grave his name was recorded on the Polish Air Force Memorial at Northolt. As the reader will have noted most of the casualties detailed within these pages, or at least the circumstances of their subsequent discovery, are often surrounded – more than just a little – by varying degrees of controversy. The case of Franciszek Gruszka is no exception.

Spitfires of 65 Squadron scramble on 13 August 1940. YT-N R6712 suffered a flying accident on 18 October. YT-M R6714 was flown by P/O Dave Glaser the previous day, when he ferried the aircraft down to the squadron's forward base at Rochford. This is listed in his flying log book. Gruszka's aircraft was R6713. Note the censor's lines through the identifiable structure in the background.

As we have seen in the previous chapter the first discovery of a previously missing Battle of Britain pilot was made in 1972, although that find was pre-dated by a little over a year with excavations carried out by the Kent Battle of Britain Museum on wreckage of a Spitfire at Grove Marshes, Westbere. Although they did not know it at the time it was in fact Spitfire R6713, the aircraft that had carried Gruszka to his death on 18 August 1940. Whilst in the 1970s the activity that latterly became known as aviation archaeology was in its infancy it was, nonetheless, a growth activity and most especially so in the south-east corner of England – the very battleground of 1940.

In these early days however the work carried out was often done with little knowledge as to the circumstances of the crash, date, pilot, aircraft type etc. Little existed then in the way of published sources of historical detail or data and access to any primary source records was limited. Very often the recovery groups then active were almost wholly reliant upon local eye-witness information and it was frequently the case that wreckages were being recovered without the faintest idea as to what the aircraft was, when it went down or even the circumstances of its loss. Such detail often only emerged with the wreckage and this indeed was the case with the Grove Marsh Spitfire. However, it is clear that some question mark hung over whether the pilot of this aeroplane had escaped or whether he had not.

Witnesses of the crash, including eleven-year-old Michael Wigmore, had seen no parachute – an ominous sign. Apparently mindful of this fact, the Kent Battle of Britain Museum requested the presence on site of police officers when an excavation eventually got underway on 28 March 1971 and the finds made during that dig were clearly indicative that indeed the pilot had not survived. Along with the Rolls-Royce Merlin engine some quantities of other wreckage were salvaged including a packed parachute and its shroud lines. The presence of an unused parachute in the cockpit of a single-seat fighter could mean only one thing.

The parachute was subsequently cleaned and displayed at the Kent Battle of Britain Museum (then located within the stately home of Chilham Castle, Kent) and identified with a caption describing the items as originating from the Spitfire of Fg Off Gruszka, an identification that had evidently been established by the aircraft serial number, R6713, stencilled onto one of the machine gun 'empties' chutes. It was not long before the question was being asked; if Gruszka is still missing and his parachute is on public display then what actually became of this airman?

As it turned out the question would be asked by two of the Polish pilot's comrades from 65 Squadron – Dave Glaser and another Pole, Boleslaw Drobinski.

By coincidence Dave Glaser was in 1974 a BAC 1-11 test pilot with British Aerospace at Hurn and worked alongside enthusiastic researcher and historian Peter Foote, then an avionics engineer for BAC. Hearing that the Kent Battle of Britain Museum were planning a re-excavation of the Grove Marsh crash site, primarily, he understood, to recover the control column, Peter Foote mentioned this fact to Glaser and pointed out that his old pal Gruszka was still officially unaccounted for.

His curiosity aroused, Glaser paid a visit to Kent to follow up reports of the 1971 recovery and to attempt to forestall any future recovery operations before he could unravel what had thus far happened. What emerged astonished him and throughout his involvement with this highly unusual case, Glaser kept detailed notes and an extensive file of reports and correspondence. We are now able to draw upon that archive to

A nineteen-year-old Pilot Officer E.D.'Dave' Glaser pictured in his Spitfire during August 1940. He joined the squadron on the same day as Brendan 'Paddy' Finucane, 13 July 1940. Finucane went on to become one of the RAF's top aces before being killed in 1942.

build up a picture of what became known amongst members of the Battle of Britain Fighter Association as the "Gruszka Affair" – a rather tawdry series of events that led to a controversial inquest and newspaper headlines like "Wreck Hunters' Lack of Respect for Dead Pilot".

On 5 March 1975 Dave Glaser made contact with the Nature Conservancy Board who controlled the Grove Marsh site and established that the 1971 dig had indeed taken place on their land but he was directed to the Ministry of Defence when suggesting that any further attempts at recovery should be barred until it could be established whether human remains were in the crash. Unfortunately, the MOD could throw no light on what had taken place in 1971 and whilst undertaking to look into the matter the ministry officials suggested that Glaser might like instead to contact the local police in the interim to see what could be done to put a stop to any future excavations. It was here that the saga of the Gruszka case took yet another and most surprising turn when Dave put in a call to Maidstone HQ of the Kent Police.

Incredibly, the officer to whom Dave Glaser was directed identified himself as a Sgt 'Ted' Baker – who was also a member of the Kent Battle of Britain Museum! As it turned out Baker knew all about the recovery in 1971, had been present during that operation and was able to make a number of interesting observations to Gruszka's former comrade-in-arms. Most importantly he divulged that Gruszka was still in the cockpit but did not know how far down one would have to dig to get him out. It would, said Baker, cost the museum £100.00 to complete the recovery and maybe Mr Glaser would like to pay for this?

Dave was astonished. Astonished that the engine and parachute had been recovered but not the pilot's body and astonished that he should now find himself being asked to fund the recovery of his dead friend! Later that same evening Baker, now off duty, telephoned Glaser to say that Gruszka was certainly in the aircraft, his body had been located and that permission had been granted for them to re-excavate the site within the next month. Nonplussed, Dave Glaser gathered his thoughts over the next day or so although it soon became clear that his conversation with Sgt Baker had been something of a catalyst. On 7 March a call from the Nature Conservancy Board confirmed that the Kent Battle of Britain Museum had indeed requested permission to re-excavate the site.

Immediately the veteran Battle of Britain pilot swung into action and by 9 April came confirmation that the RAF's No 71 Maintenance Unit, based at Bicester, had been detailed to carry out the recovery of the pilot's body although one member only of the Kent Battle of Britain Museum was authorised to be present. It was to be a 'Priority 1' tasking for 71 MU. At last it seemed that officialdom had taken control and had a grasp on the situation. Or had it?

By Monday 14 April, a Royal Engineer party were due on site to drain away water with the recovery scheduled to start on Wednesday the 16th. However, on the Tuesday the Nature Conservancy Board had telephoned Glaser to say that they were surprised to find that recovery work had already started that morning with twelve of the museum team present and the operation apparently being led by Sgt Baker although one RAF corporal (Cpl P J Law), one royal engineer and four airmen were also present. Baker, although not on duty, evidently wore his police cap to show some form of authority. Unhappy at the developing situation the Nature Conservancy officer, Mr Phillips, entered into some altercation with Sgt Baker who responded that they had the authority to carry out the dig although Phillips insisted this was not so and only one of their number were authorised to be present.

The situation on the crash site was now wholly out of the control of Cpl Law who was supposed to be in charge of the operation, although with the excavation now fully underway the mechanical digger soon unearthed the expected human remains and the East Kent coroner's officer, PC Tudor, was called to attend. It was at this point that Tudor reiterated that the museum group had authority for only one person to be present although Baker, no doubt using his senior rank, insisted to PC Tudor that two of their number should remain. With order finally restored the work got underway again with Cpl Law in charge. By the day's end the remains of the pilot had been wholly recovered along with a Mae West, note book, parachute harness and Polish pilot's wings along with a further quantity of aircraft wreckage.

When an inquest was finally convened in Canterbury during May 1975, it was under the auspices of Dr Wilfred Mowll and the proceedings were followed avidly by the local and national press. Here was an extremely unusual story with ingredients of high wartime drama, tragedy and controversy all rolled into one. At the very outset it was clear from the line taken by Dr Mowll that he was less than happy with how matters had proceeded both during the 1971 and 1975 excavations. After taking formal evidence of identification, and hearing the evidence of Dr Alexander Ogilvy the pathologist, Dr Mowll adjourned the inquest for three weeks in order that he could go further into the question of the 1971 dig. On 29 May 1975 the inquest was duly re-convened in Canterbury Sessions House.

The first witness called was Michael Llewellyn, described as founder and curator of the Kent Battle of Britain Museum. It was again obvious from the very outset that Dr Mowll was intent on a very aggressive line of questioning and it emerged during the hearing that teeth had in fact been found during the first excavation in 1971. It was clearly a matter that exercised Dr Mowll greatly. Questioned about the pilot's body, Llewellyn confirmed that "no body as such" was found although parts of a tunic and some teeth were discovered. The teeth, it emerged, were consigned back to the hole. Asking "Why did you discard the teeth?" Dr Mowll received a terse reply from Llewellyn: "They were put back in the hole as a mark of respect," to which the coroner retorted "That's not very nice, is it? Put back in a muddy hole?"

Backwards and forwards the argument raged, with Llewellyn claiming that the remains were re-buried with the knowledge of police officers present although when called to give evidence one of those officers, Superintendent Fenn, denied emphatically any knowledge of the discovery of teeth. Fenn went on to state, quite logically, that given the discovery of a rudder pedal it was surprising to him that no body was found if the pilot was indeed still on board. That find, coupled with the seat type parachute, one might reasonably assume to be associated to and in close proximity of any occupant of the Spitfire. And yet Fenn was unaware that any such finds had been made.

Clearly displeased, the coroner moved matters forward to the 1975 dig and accused Llewellyn of assuming authority over Corporal Lord. It was a point that Llewellyn refuted, suggesting instead that he had merely helped Corporal Law to locate the precise spot where the plane had crashed. Either way, other witnesses were not happy and one, Boleslaw

Drobinski, asked why and how it was that with Gruszka only found and identified in 1975 there had been a parachute hanging up in the Chilham Castle Museum long before then with the name of Gruszka beneath it?

Llewellyn explained how that identification had been achieved in 1971 by cross-checking records with the serial number discovered on the machine-gun chute although Drobinski, Glaser and Dr Mowll were all critical of the fact that the authorities had not been informed of any link to a missing man, and with Glaser especially concerned that Gruszka's relatives could have chanced upon discovering this detail had they visited the museum. That said, and to be fair to the recovery group, no formal guidelines then existed to cover such eventualities. The museum had been groping in the dark – both when delving in the muddy crater at Westbere and when exhibiting their finds.

Ultimately, it fell to Dr Mowll to pronounce that Flying Officer Gruszka had died through injuries caused during war service. He went on:

"On 18 August 1940, for reasons not accounted for, he dived into the marshes. It is a moving story and one must do honour to this man. I hope I have done so.

"Arising out of it has been the perhaps unfortunate recovery of the engine but not the body in 1971. Mr Llewellyn's evidence about the interring of the teeth has been challenged by the police and they were there with the express purpose of reporting anything found. I must adhere to the line I took that in fact no part of the body was found – unless Mr Llewellyn did find the teeth which makes the story even more unpleasant."

Dr Mowll then went on to draw attention to the Ministry of Defence Notes of Guidance for Aircraft Recovery Groups. Implicit within his comments was the clear indication that the Kent Battle of Britain Museum ought to have been minded as to the contents of that guidance note. It was an entirely fatuous statement. The note of guidance had not been issued until 1974 – three years *after* the initial dig! And it had no relevance, either, to the 1974 recovery which was officially an RAF-led operation.

All in all it was a sorry state of affairs and the events that had taken place and the proceedings of the inquest gave plenty of column inches for the press to make some mileage out of what became a rather murky tale. All said and done though it is necessary to view the events of 1971 in the light of experiences of any recovery group up to that date in discovering missing aircrew. Quite simply there were none. This was uncharted territory and the first missing pilot discovered in the UK was Pilot Officer George James Drake (see Chapter Two) who was not found until 1972. There must have been some anxiety on the part of the Kent Battle of Britain Museum when approaching the dig at Grove Marsh and having learned that the pilot may not have escaped. That is why, apparently, police officers were present on the 1971 dig….just in case.

One must also take into account the defence of the museum team in relation to that 1971 dig, to wit: that the museum was uncertain as to its legal, moral or religious obligations. Indeed, once they had suspected human remains were present when the recovery group found the parachute, it is certainly understandable that some consternation arose which then led to the immediate closing down of further digging operations. Playing devil's advocate, one has to consider why it was that the museum did not discount any excavation at the Gruszka site in the first place, given possible complications that might arise. There were at the time, after all, plenty more aircraft wreck sites from 1940 to be found in Kent that would not present such problems! Further, it is certainly the case that the team subsequently re-appraised their position and were later ready to re-excavate the site in 1975. Whatever the truth of the matter the furore that blew up and that is still talked about perhaps rather obscured the more important aspect of the whole case – and that is doing full justice to the pilot, Franciszek Gruszka. We should leave it to his friend Boleslaw Drobinski to paint us a brief portrait of the man:

"By the end of January 1940 when I arrived in England there were about two hundred fully trained Polish pilots at Eastchurch all eager to go on conversion courses, all wanting to fly with the RAF and all wanting to be ready when the phoney war would be over and the real one would begin. Unfortunately, because of the language difficulties and other things it was not until June 1940, just about the time of the collapse of France, that serious flying training started.

"During that frustrating period of waiting when the time was almost equally divided between English lessons, playing bridge, ground parades and biting our nails I remember that Gruszka, being just as eager to fly as the next man, was at least more cheerful than most of us and very often his sense of humour was a very welcome relief in otherwise more monotonous day to day life. He was liked by almost everybody and easy to get along with.

"Gruszka graduated from the Polish Air Force College in Deblin near Warsaw as a 2nd Lt in 1934 and was promoted to Lt in 1937 serving then as a senior pilot and instructor in the 6th Polish Air Force Regiment at Lwow. Here, he married a girl called Eugene but when the war in Poland was over he, like many others, escaped from the country and ended up at RAF Eastchurch on the Isle of Sheppey.

One of Gruszka's fellow Polish pilots in 65 Squadron was Boleslaw Drobinski. He arrived at the squadron on 12 August 1940 and is seen wearing the Polish airforce emblem below his RAF wings. Drobinski along with Dave Glaser and Jeffrey Quill were instrumental in getting the RAF to undertake the second excavation of the crash-site to try and locate Gruszka's remains.

"It is not surprising therefore that I was very pleased to find myself in the same squadron (No 65) in which Szulkowski and Gruszka were serving. I found Gruszka to be exactly the same as I remembered him from Eastchuch and I also found that he was liked by everybody in the squadron. He made friends easily and there was a young Pilot Officer, Dave Glaser, who became Gruszka's close friend and was teaching him English. In turn, Gruszka was trying to teach him some Polish! Altogether there was a feeling of great friendliness in the squadron and so we, the Poles, especially appreciated it. So, when on 18 August 1940 Gruszka was posted missing there was a genuine sadness in the whole squadron."

Exactly what happened to cause the loss of Flying Officer Gruszka remains open to speculation. As we have seen, and apparently according to at least some RAF records, he was last spotted in pursuit of enemy aircraft at 14.50hrs that day and this was certainly the timing given under oath to Dr Mowll at the inquest by MOD official Mr Kenneth Wall. However, a discrepancy emerges here because the operations record book states that Gruszka was one of six aircraft that took off from Rochford at 12.50 that day with five aircraft (minus Gruszka) returning at 14.00hrs. Consequently, if these timings are accurate then one might assess the crash at Westbere that took Gruszka's life should have been at some time around 13.30hrs.

This timing would certainly make much more sense when looking at the overall operational picture of what was going on that day. If accurate, then a time around 13.30hrs lends itself to being linked with a number of possible German fighter claims in the right area and at the right time. Equally, his loss might well have been down to some other form of mechanical malfunction or even some temporary medical incapacity. Possible reasons for the loss of this aeroplane and its pilot are legion, although it is also a fact that the pathologist, Dr Ogilvie, was unable to say whether the pilot had been killed by bullets or cannon fire as there were no signs of this nature visible on the remains he examined. The absence of such evidence, however, does not mean one can exclude that as the cause of death. It is important, also, that another controversial element is dealt with here and dispensed with.

Michael Wigmore, then an eleven-year-old boy, was a witness to the crash and lived nearby at Link Cottage. Before the crash he thought that he had heard gunfire but could not be sure although the aeroplane simply dived into the marsh at a forty-five degree angle and buried itself on impact with the soft soil. Immediately after the crash, another Spitfire was seen to circle around before flying off and a local rumour had persisted that this was a case of Spitfire v. Spitfire. The rumour is further embellished with tales of a feud between two pilots and of a pre-arranged duel taking place, although it has to be said that not a shred of evidence has ever emerged to support this rather wild theory.

Of course, a genuine case of accidental friendly fire could always be a possibility and such events were certainly relatively common. However, no evidence for a friendly fire case has emerged, either, in this particular instance but one might speculate, of course, that the "circling Spitfire" story coupled with a possibly inaccurate time of 14.50hrs that does not fit any German fighter claims merely feeds the friendly fire rumour mill for some. The story of Gruszka's loss does not, in the view of the author, constitute any sinister mystery although correspondence from aviation author Frank Mason during October 1975 to Dave Glaser after the furore had all but died down perhaps touched upon the matter again. He wrote:

"....there is just one other thing I must add. The fire may have been put out, but I am very worried that a single most dangerous spark still exists. Any further wind could fan the whole thing into an awful blaze. Bob (Stanford Tuck) may, if he thinks fit, be more explicit. I hope not."

After lying in the wreck of his Spitfire for almost forty years, Gruszka was finally laid to rest at Northwood Cemetery on 17 July 1975 with full military honours. This sequence of pictures is representative of an RAF funeral with full military honours.

If Dave Glaser ever knew what it was to which Mason was rather obliquely referring then there is no hint of this within his extensive archive on the subject. However, if Bob Stanford Tuck was not explicit in explaining things to Glaser then he was certainly more than explicit to this author when the matter was touched upon in 1979. He wrote:

"…the whole Gruszka affair was a bloody shambles. Things went on that should not have gone on, that much is clear. I am afraid too that there were those lurking around in the background with some kind of intent to stir up a fuss about how poor old Gruszka was done for. Stupid stories about how he had been shot down. Now, I am pretty much of the view that this might have been aimed at causing some pain for those of the Battle of Britain Fighter Association who had been asking difficult questions of some people. I don't know, but I hope not. Absolute tosh, really."

At every turn the story about the post-war discovery of Flying Officer Gruszka has confronted controversy but his eventual burial by the RAF amongst brother Poles at Northwood Cemetery on Thursday 17 July 1975 at least drew some kind of a line under this convoluted tale. Certainly it is fitting and appropriate that this Polish airman was reverentially laid to rest in a marked grave and that his status was finally removed from the list of those classified as missing. That said, there had been an appealingly simple charm to the practice of Mr & Mrs Wigmore's daughters laying flowers at the crash site during the second week of every August. Simple posies among the stark wilderness that is Grove Marsh. Until 1975 his name had been unknown to them. Unknown maybe. But certainly not forgotten.

CHAPTER 7

The Discovery of Hugh Beresford

THE DISCOVERY of Flying Officer Gruszka had attracted both controversy and media attention – a common thread to be found running through almost all of the cases detailed in this book. The case of Hugh Beresford, though, attracted a brighter spotlight than most for on 7 September 1980 BBC2 Television screened its documentary "Missing" as part of its Inside Story series of programmes. The date was significant for it was exactly forty years to the day since the subject of that programme, Flt Lt Hugh Beresford, was shot down and killed in action. Now, we can look in an historical context at both the circumstances of his loss in action and the events surrounding the discovery of both Beresford and his Hurricane.

It is no secret that 257 (Burma) Squadron was considered to have been poorly led during the early part of the Battle of Britain and at a low ebb in terms of morale. Flt Lt Geoff Myers pulled no punches when he

Flt Lt Hugh Richard Aden Beresford of 257 Squadron.

wrote in his diary of the desperate state that 257 Squadron was in. Fiercely critical of the CO (Sqn Ldr H Harkness) he tells how the squadron was more or less held together by the two well respected flight commanders, Fg Off 'Lance' Mitchell and Flt Lt Hugh Beresford. Of Beresford, Myers wrote how exhaustion was taking its toll, of a nervous twitch and how he would obsessively pace the dispersal hut asking "What's the time?" and "I'm sure there will be a Blitz soon". To his fellow pilots, and particularly to the NCOs, he was known affectionately as 'Blue-Blood Beresford'; a reference to his aristocratic good looks and

Beresford had been a pre-war regular pilot and had served with 3 Squadron at RAF Kenley flying Bristol Bulldogs. He is pictured here, seated on a chair fourth from the right, during a squadron group photograph.

bearing. As the A Flight commander he had been in action almost daily throughout the battle and on 18 August 1940 he had shot down a He 111, shared with Sgt Girdwood. On the fateful day of 7 September 1940, Beresford had already been up with the squadron three times when the final call to scramble came in.

At 16.35hrs the squadron's Hurricanes roared away from RAF Martlesham Heath vectored onto a large enemy formation approaching up the Thames Estuary. Head on, the Hurricanes approached a formation of about fifty bombers but an escort of fighters above fell on the squadron as they attacked. By calling a frantic warning: "ALERT squadron – four snappers coming down – now!" *(ALERT being the radio call sign for 257 Squadron)*, Beresford had tried to warn the others of danger from four diving Me109s. He called that he couldn't attack because another Hurricane was in his way. Then silence. Nothing more was seen of Hugh Beresford until the discovery of his Hurricane in 1979.

Far below the confused mass of fighters and bombers, River Board worker Ashley Read went about his daily chores inspecting the water courses that criss-cross the Isle of Sheppey in Kent. Watching the dogfight developing above in a rising crescendo of engine noise and rattling machine guns, he saw a lone Hurricane fall away from the battle. Following its progress he watched as it entered a headlong dive; waiting, expecting and hoping that the pilot would leave his obviously stricken fighter. By the time the Hurricane was in a vertical attitude, and now at only a few hundred feet, Ashley realised he was witnessing the awful finality of a young pilot's life. With a terrible thud which shook the very ground on which he stood, the Hurricane impacted a few hundred feet away alongside a ditch at Spit End Point, Elmley.

Suddenly, there was silence. The air battle above had moved away, or dispersed, and the peace and tranquillity of Sheppey had returned. Only the twitter of skylarks seemed to break the silence, contrasting with the noise of battle just moments before. When the Hurricane had impacted there was no fire, no explosion and no bullets cracking-off in the heat of an inferno. Ashley walked across to the spot. There seemed no point in running.

21793 W1.33405/3503 400,000 12/39—McC & Co—51-5658

				References to Appendices
R.A.F. Form 540.			OPERATIONS RECORD BOOK	Page No. 3
See instructions for use of this form in K.R. and A.C.I., para. 2349, and War Manual, Pt. II., chapter XX., and notes in R.A.F. Pocket Book.			of (Unit or Formation) 257 (BURMA) SQUADRON	No. of pages used for day

Place	Date	Time	Summary of Events	References to Appendices
			sections. From 13.00 hrs "A" Flight were released & "B" Flight remained at 30 mins. availability. Two patrols were carried out.	
	6-9-40		At 11-30 "B" Flight patrolled MARTLESHAM at 15,000 ft. At 12.53 "A" Flight which was ~~ready~~ released until 13.00 hrs. was called to readiness. At 13-00 hrs. "B" Flight left MARTLESHAM & patrolled GRAVESEND at 20,000 ft. At 13-10 hrs. "A" Flight took off on the same patrol. No enemy aircraft were seen. A last patrol was carried out over CHELMSFORD at 20000 ft from 17-30 to 18-50 hrs.	
	7-9-40		"A" Flight patrolled MARTLESHAM twice during the morning. At 11-15 the whole Squadron took off & patrolled COLCHESTER at 15,000 ft landing at 12-20. At 14-15 the whole Squadron was called to readiness from 15 mins. availability. At 16-50 the Squadron left MARTLESHAM to patrol CHELMSFORD at 17,000 ft Under the command of S/LDR. HARKNESS it was sectored to the ROCHESTER area. The Squadron intercepted a formation of about 50 enemy bombers flying up the THAMES ESTUARY. The bombers were escorted by a great number of fighters flying above them. In the ensuing combat F/LT BERESFORD "A" Flight commander & P/O MITCHELL "B" Flight commander were lost & posted as missing. RFRT succeeded in making a	

Details of all operations carried out by RAF squadrons were entered in the operations record book, or Form 540. Losses sustained by the squadron were noted, as here in the case of Flt Lt Beresford and Fg Off Mitchell, although the facts were scant and cold. Little can ever be found in these record books to help pinpoint exactly where missing casualties were actually lost.

Arriving at the scene he was amazed by what he saw. Great clods of soil and clay had been thrown around a black stain of the smallest of craters. Two slashes in the grass either side marked the impact point of the wings. Just the tiniest wisp of steam or smoke emerged from fissures in the surrounding ground. Of the 'plane itself only tiny shards of silver, brown and green alloy were in evidence. "Barely enough," in the words of Ashley "to even half fill an apple box!"

Back at Martlesham Heath the remnants of the squadron began to lick its collective wounds. Three pilots had failed to return; Beresford, Mitchell and Sgt Hulbert, although news later came through that Hulbert was OK and had crash-landed near Sittingbourne. Of the two flight commanders, though, there was no news and enquiries to other airfields, police HQs and the observer corps all drew blanks. The other pilots could shed no light either on what had happened for nobody had seen the going of either Beresford or Mitchell. All had been too busy taking care of their own survival to notice anything. It was indeed the blackest of days for 257 Squadron and Geoffrey Myers was moved to write in his diary:

Geoffrey Myers, the 257 Squadron Intelligence Officer, watches a game of chess at dispersal. It was Myers who recalled the loss of Hugh Beresford on 7 September 1940 and the reaction of the adjutant to Pat Beresford's tearful telephone calls. The pilot seated on the edge of the table is thought to be Lance Mitchell, the other flight commander posted missing with Beresford.

"Hugh Beresford. Another hero gone. Mrs Beresford rang up last night. She was in tears. The Adjutant tried to soothe her over the telephone. He didn't quite know what he was saying. Spoke to her about boats that might have picked Beresford up at sea. He told her not to give up hope, but she knew. She asked if she could fetch his clothes. 'She sounds sweet,' the adjutant said. He was almost in tears himself. He had a double whisky after that."

Five days later the CO was posted away to Boscombe Down and in October appointed CO of No 2 Squadron, 10 Flying Training School. He did not fly operationally again. Later, in 1943, he resigned his commission. In Larry Forrester's book *Fly For Your Life*, an account is given of how Bob Stanford Tuck was posted in to take command of the Squadron on 11 September and to sort out what amounted to a most frightful mess.

With no immediate indication as to his fate, Hugh Beresford was simply classified as missing in action. Accordingly, the standard telegram was sent out to his young widow, Pat, to tell her in cold and stark Air Ministry-speak that he had failed to return from an operational flight and that she would be contacted as soon as there was other news. That news was never forthcoming and one year after his death he was presumed dead for official purposes.

On 7 September 1940, during the same action that saw the loss of Beresford and Mitchell, Sgt D J Hulbert was also shot down but safely made a forced-landing. Although this is not Hulbert's aeroplane, photographs of 257 Squadron Hurricanes of the period are hard to source – hence the inclusion of this image.

Back at his home village of Hoby in Leicestershire, Hugh's father (the vicar of Hoby), his mother and sister Pamela were distraught at the loss of a much loved son and brother. Hugh had been the last male in the Beresford line and the family had lived in Hoby for centuries. With the death of Pamela in 1990 the family line finally ended. Pat, Hugh's young widow, re-married one of her late husband's best chums – Wing Commander 'Hughie' Edwards VC DSO DFC. Post-war the couple emigrated to Australia where he became the Governor of Western Australia. Sadly, Pat died in 1966 never knowing what had become of her first husband.

Shortly after Ashley Read had watched the Hurricane plunge into the ground, personnel from nearby RAF Eastchurch came across to the crash site. Little could be done however, but the crash was reported to the RAF Maintenance Unit serving the south-east, 49 MU at RAF Faygate. The job of salvage at Spit End was tasked out to civilian contractors, A V Nicholls & Co, a Brighton-based haulage firm. With his company detailed for the recovery of the Hurricane, Arthur Nicholls himself visited the crash site filing the report (on the next page) to Squadron Leader Goodman at Faygate.

To the RAF salvage organisation this was just another wrecked Hurricane and its location, coupled with the fact that it was obviously very deeply buried, resulted in no further action being taken to effect its recovery. After Nicholls submitted his report, there the matter rested. Officially there appeared to be nothing to link the Spit End incident with the loss of Hugh Beresford. Or was there?

HURRICANE.   Spit End, Elmley, Sheppey.

       The above aircraft has crashed in marshy land a mile
and a half from the nearest hard road. Flight Sergeant Bishop
of the R.A.F. stationed at Eastchurch accompanied me to a point
near to the crash. It was impossible to get on the site of
the crash owing to the state of the marsh; it was raining hard
at the time. There is no road track leading to the site of
this crash and it will be necessary for the vehicle removing
the aircraft to travel over the marsh. Flight Sergeant Bishop
says this would be impossible until the marsh is quite dry and
hard. It will also be necessary for the vehicle to negotiate
a gradiant of 1 in 3 after it is loaded. It would appear that
a Tractor is most suitable for this clearance. I suggest as
an alternative that the R.A.F. stationed at Eastchurch, might
drag this wreckage across the marsh by means of their Bren Gun
Carrier, the lorry then picking it up from the edge of the
marsh. I await your instructions for further action.

                 Signed ____ *A.W.Nicholls*

Flt Lt Hugh Beresford's Hurricane had been shot down at Spit End Point, Isle of Sheppey, although no evidence linking him to the crash was established when the site was visited by Air Ministry contractor Arthur Nicholls. Here is Nicholls's inconclusive report. In 1979 it would become possible to establish a firm and definite link to Beresford.

Writing to Hugh's father on 17 September 1940, Air Vice-Marshal Ernest Gossage told how Beresford had once been his personal assistant at Uxbridge and, during that time, he had become very fond of him. The condolence letter went on to say that: "I wanted to be sure that no possibility existed of him being alive before I wrote to extend our sincere and heartfelt sympathy." As Air Member for Personnel at the Air Ministry, Gossage was surely better placed than anyone to have available the most accurate and up-to-date material relating to RAF casualties.

Did he have some information, perhaps, that confirmed the wrecked Hurricane at Spit End to be Beresford's aircraft, P3049? Did he also, perhaps, have information that confirmed the pilot had not baled out? Either way, the most senior ranked officer in the RAF dealing with personnel, and also in overall charge of the RAF's casualty branch, was quite clearly telling Hugh Beresford's father that his son was certainly dead – and just ten days after the event! Best, maybe, not to tell the family the awful truth that their son's body could not be recovered and that it lay in deeply embedded wreckage beneath remote marshland? On the other hand, if the Air Ministry did know the truth Hugh Beresford remained officially listed as missing and his wife and family continued to endure the agony of uncertainty.

Indeed, right up until 1979 his sister, Pamela, had clung to some hope that one day her brother might walk through the

Hugh Beresford with his bride, Pat, on their wedding day. When Flight Lieutenant Hugh Beresford was posted missing on 7 September 1940, Pat repeatedly telephoned the squadron adjutant for news of his whereabouts. There was none.

door – even keeping some his things ready in case he should return. After forty years that might sound irrational, and yet on the other hand it is easy to understand that there had been no finality. Eventually however there would be a turn of events that would put the whole matter – and Hugh himself – to final rest.

At some point during the early 1970s enthusiasts had twice excavated on the Spit End site. At least one of those excavations had been by the Kent Battle of Britain Museum when evidence had come to light that the aeroplane was indeed a Hurricane and, more significantly, the Form 700 aircraft log book had been found. This, together with airframe

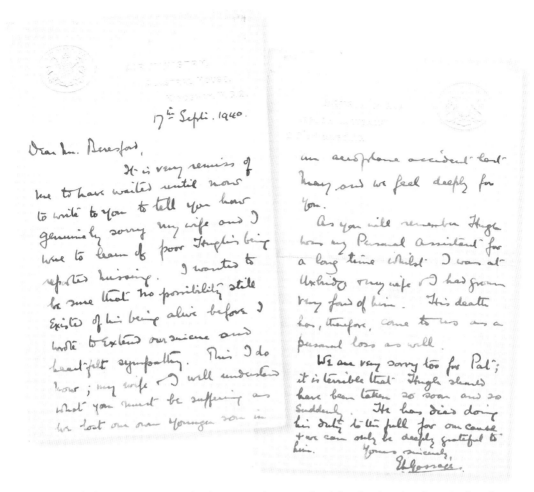

Air Vice-Marshal Gossage wrote this letter to the Beresford family shortly after Hugh's disappearance and its content seems to suggest that, somehow, Gossage then had confirmation that Hugh Beresford was dead. It is unclear how he might have come to such a firm conclusion so soon after Beresford had failed to return.

components bearing the serial number P3049, provided proof-positive as to what had become of Flt Lt Beresford. In fact, the salvaged artefacts were placed on display at Chilham Castle and identified as being from Hugh's Hurricane. Thus his hitherto mysterious fate had been placed in the public domain, just as in the case of Fg Off Gruszka. Sadly, Pamela Beresford remained unaware.

Indeed, as the controversy over Gruszka raged on in correspondence between Dave Glaser, Bob Stanford Tuck, 'Mac' McDonnell and Jeffrey Quill of the Battle of Britain Fighter Association so the subject of Hugh Beresford's earlier excavation by the Chilham group arose. "There is the question," wrote Quill on 21 July 1975 "of what should now be done in the case of Beresford where there seems at least a possibility that the body has been discovered but left in the crater." Dave Glaser, in his response, expressed concern that there was again a case where artefacts associated with a still-missing pilot were on public view, going on to state: "…there is no need for me to point out the public outcry that would arise should a relative happen to visit the museum." As things turned out, subsequent events rather overtook the possibility of any unexpected Beresford family visits to Chilham.

With the knowledge that both previous excavations had failed to recover the wreckage, or indeed the missing pilot, the now disbanded Wealden Aviation Archaeological Group decided to make one further attempt. Coinciding with this renewed interest in the site, BBC2 Television had been seeking the recovery of a Battle of Britain aircraft as the subject for an *Inside Story* documentary. To producer Peter Gordon the Beresford case seemed an ideal subject. Accordingly, on 29 September 1979 the deeply buried wreckage was recovered for the cameras. Surprisingly, the previous excavations were found to have extended to a depth further than the buried wreckage – but as we now know very little of the Hurricane was recovered during the previous digs although the discovery of the aircraft travelling log book and the radio mast had indicated likely excavation in close proximity to the cockpit area. Not surprisingly, the unfortunate pilot was found still in his aircraft during the 1979 recovery and Flt Lt Hugh Richard Aden Beresford, 31750, aged 24, was no longer missing.

When the crash site was fully excavated in September 1979 it became possible positively to confirm that this was where Hugh Beresford's Hurricane, P3049, had crashed and also to establish the fate of this long-missing airman. His tattered identity card helped to underline the fact that the mystery of his disappearance had at last been solved.

It has to be said that with the wonderful benefit of hindsight those involved in the 1979 recovery would have done things very differently thirty years on. In the case of Hugh Beresford (and indeed other such recoveries) the family was presented with a *fait accompli* after the recovery had taken place. With more careful research and planning it would have been possible to trace Pamela Beresford and present her with the facts and leave the choice of recovery, or not, entirely up to her. Any reservations about how the Beresford case was finally treated, including the television programme, might be tempered with the knowledge that Pamela's mind was finally put to rest – along with her hero brother. Had he remained missing it is less than likely that anyone would know anything of this man – who he was, what he looked like, what he did or how he died. Most certainly he would not have had national and international press and TV exposure. His would simply have been a name carved amongst more than 20,000 at the Runnymede Memorial.

Finally, on 16 November 1979, Hugh Beresford was laid to rest with full military honours in Brookwood Military Cemetery, Surrey. The Central Band of the RAF and The Queens Colour Squadron provided the honours. Speaking at his funeral, Air Chief Marshal Sir Christopher Foxley-Norris said of Beresford: "For a moment in time he held the whole future of civilisation in his two sweating palms and did not let it go." His discovery, almost forty years after being lost, enabled more than just epithets and epitaths.

The Flight Lieutenant

In the marsh the curlews cry
Beneath the empty bowl of sky,
Beneath the sun and flying cloud
Earth my grave and mud my shroud.
For forty years I've quietly lain
In the wreckage of my 'plane.
Baled out, they said, or lost at sea
But no-one came in search of me.
A distant ploughman drives his team,
And rushes rattle in the stream:
In summer time the cattle tread
Heavy-footed overhead.
Yet somehow in these bones I know
Man will devise machines that show
Where metal lies, and he will trace
My 'plane in its last resting place.
Then will the lonely waiting cease
And these tired bones will rest at peace.

K D Clarke
(Inspired by the loss and subsequent discovery of
Flt Lt Hugh Beresford at Spit End, Elmley, Isle of Sheppey)

CHAPTER 8

One of The Few and One of The Best

I N ALL probability the case of Hurricane pilot Pilot Officer John Ramsay, missing in action on 18 August 1940, would not have had the ending it did, or ever been solved, were it not for a remarkable chance discovery by the author. Idly scanning the *Daily Telegraph* announcements column dated 22 June 1981 the author's eye fell on the following:

> "RAMSAY – On June 16 1981. Peacefully at Poole Hospital, Esme Sarah, widow of C. Allan Ramsay of Bombay and mother of John, Pilot Officer, lost in the Battle of Britain 1940."

It was an uncanny and extraordinary coincidence since enthusiast Steve Vizard had only recently located the approximate crash site of a Hurricane at Holiwell Point, Burnham on Crouch, Essex. Research pointed to this aircraft being the Hurricane flown by Pilot Officer J B Ramsay of 151 Squadron who had been lost in action on

Pilot Officer John Basil Ramsay was just twenty-one years old when he disappeared on 18 August 1940 – the hardest fought day of the Battle of Britain.

18 August 1940. He was still missing. Percy Chapman of Middlewick Farm had seen the crash on what was now John Yeldham's land and he was certain that nobody had escaped. Mr Yeldham himself, then only five, was also of the same view – that the pilot had gone down with the aircraft. Despite their recollections, it was the hard evidence of reports from the 6th Anti-Aircraft Division that helped point towards Pilot Officer Ramsay being the pilot concerned.

According to the Ministry of Defence, and even if the date of crash at Holiwell Point could be established as 18 August 1940, this did not necessarily point to Pilot Officer Ramsay. On the same day, and at roughly the same time, Flt Lt 'Dickie' Lee of 85 Squadron had vanished in this particular Hurricane, P2923.

In the detailed intelligence report of the division it was stated that at some time just after 1700hrs a Hurricane had crashed at Holiwell Point and quoted a map reference, 471146. A quick check with wartime ordnance survey maps revealed that this map reference corresponded closely to the position where messrs Chapman and Yeldham had recalled the crash. Given that other reports in the same document related to other *known* crashes, where the pilots were identified, the Holiwell Point incident clearly had a question mark hanging over who the pilot was and what had happened to him.

As to the pilot, there were only two possibilities: Plt Off J B Ramsey 151 Squadron or Flt Lt R H A 'Dickie' Lee of 85 Squadron. Both were shot down at around 1700 on 18 August. Both were still missing. In the case of Lee, however, he was last seen chasing enemy aircraft some thirty miles off the coast. Ramsay seemed the only contender who might really be considered and the incident at Holiwell corresponded, geographically, to where Ramsay was last seen and also to where the squadron had been engaged in action. Indeed, 151 Squadron's commanding officer had been shot down nearby in the same battle.

Taking the matter forward at Holiwell Point was, however, something that greatly exercised Steve Vizard and his team. Previously criticised for undertaking recoveries that had resulted in the discovery of missing pilots (eg Sgt Brimble) it was decided that this case ought only to be moved forward with the consent of any surviving next of kin. The problem was that none had been found. Consequently, the project foundered. Foundered, that is, until the chance discovery of the *Daily Telegraph* announcement.

Working from that almost inconsequential insert in the newspaper, the author was able almost immediately to make contact with the Ramsay family. Years had depleted the family line, and it emerged that with the loss of John in 1940 the male line had died out. The only living relatives were now his cousins, Miss Joan Worth and Lt Cdr Peter Worth. Joan very much took the lead in what would then unfold and was impressed by the research carried out that, in her view, conclusively pointed to her cousin John still being with his Hurricane at Burnham on Crouch. Armed with the research material presented to her, Joan met with those in charge of the RAF's casualty branch (then Department AR9 of the MOD) to press for formal action to recover John from the wreck. Whilst helpful and sympathetic, the branch declined to take any further action and suggested to Joan that the evidence for supposing the Holiwell crash to be John's was "flimsy". On the other hand, the MOD were not willing to sanction a private recovery at the crash site because "…there are circumstances that prompt the MOD to decide that it is better the site should not be disturbed."

Joan Worth, however, was unhappy to leave matters be. She was single-mindedly determined and headstrong in forging ahead with what she considered to be the right thing to do. Herself a very senior civil servant at the Home Office, she well understood the machinations of government departments and was certainly not cowed by them. What she decided to do was motivated by what she knew her aunt, John's mother, had always longed and wished for. One way or another every attempt must be made to bring John home. As she herself stated:

This modification data plate was found by the author lying in one of the expansive fields at Holiwell Point in Essex during March 1983. It was the first positive proof that a Hurricane had crashed here, but was unhelpful in identifying the specific aeroplane or pilot. That evidence was buried deep beneath the ground.

"The establishment is hard to beat, even when you are part of it. The MOD need to hold onto their 'policy' come what may."

With an absolute clarity of purpose, she asked Steve Vizard and his team to go ahead and recover the Hurricane notwithstanding the MOD's clearly expressed wishes. She would stand behind them come what may.

On 6 March 1983 that plan moved one stage further with the exact pinpointing of the crash site. Field-walking the massive featureless fields at Holiwell Point the author found an alloy modifications plate on the surface of the crop-sewn ground. It was from a Hurricane. In itself the plate told nothing of the history of this specific aeroplane nor of the pilot that had flown it. But a Hurricane had certainly crashed here. Journeying to the site, Joan Worth's mind was made up. She felt that she knew John was here. And he couldn't be left.

John Yeldham, the farmer, agreed and was compliant with the request to excavate after the coming harvest.

The penultimate act in bringing John home was the excavation laid on for 11 August 1983 when a large mechanical excavator was moved to the site by Steve's team. In a matter of hours it was all over. The wreckage had been recovered, smashed but with the metalwork well-preserved, from a depth of over twenty feet. As expected, the pilot was in the cockpit and Essex Police were duly called to the site and the remains removed by the coroner's instructions. The formality of identity was made easy by the discovery of the aircraft constructor's plate bearing the serial number R4181 known to be the Hurricane in which John had been lost. The said plate was duly handed over to the authorities for use in any formal identification process. Intermingled with the wreckage were various other clues including documents and still-legible paperwork bearing John's name, including some of his visiting cards. Most poignant of all was a gold cygnet ring engraved JBR and, on its inside, the date of his recent 21st birthday.

The recovery of John Ramsay and his Hurricane finally took place during August 1983. Here, the topsoil is carefully removed during the recovery operation. On the horizon is the sea wall, with the North Sea beyond. The photograph illustrates well the size of the fields that had to be searched and the difficulties associated with such investigations when researchers are faced with scant information to locate the actual crash site.

An incredible find was Pilot Officer John Ramsay's parachute. When exposed to the brisk east-coast wind the parachute billowed open and to the amazement of the recovery team was in near-perfect condition. What a tragedy that John Ramsay had not seen the comforting sight of this blossoming parachute above him on 18 August 1940.

So much for evidence that this was where John crashed being in any way "flimsy". That said, it may well have been his commanding officer's testimony that caused some doubt to be cast in official minds. In March 1941 he wrote to John's grieving parents from the RAF Hospital, Torquay, where he was recovering from wounds received during that 18 August battle:

"Dear Mr & Mrs Ramsay,

Thank you for your letter. I'm afraid that I can't give you much information concerning John. He was flying with me, that is, in my section on August 18. We met some Heinkel 111s just south of Chelmsford and they turned about and flew back east when they saw us. I believe that there were a number of fighters who came down on us from above and hit John and myself. I took to my parachute and landed in the River Crouch about two or three miles inland from the coast. The engagement however did continue out to sea.

I am very sorry I can't give you more information. Nor can I honestly offer you any great hope if the Air Ministry cannot do so, but I do think that it could have been possible for John to have reached the French or Belgian coast.

I was very sorry indeed when I heard John was missing. John was very keen and capable and we all liked him very much. I had great hopes for him and can only offer my deepest sympathy and hope that perhaps you will hear good news soon.

Yours sincerely

J A Gordon (Squadron Leader)"

Perhaps, then, this slight doubt about whether John went down in the sea or not, as expressed by his commanding officer, had some bearing when the MOD looked at the case for Joan Worth in the 1980s? Either way, there were only two missing pilots who were in the frame; Lee and Ramsay. Lee had certainly last been *seen* over the North Sea, pursuing enemy aircraft some thirty miles off the coast. Ramsey had last been seen overland in the Chelmsford area.

As a service pilot John could, nevertheless, have probably sat out the war in *relative* safety. Upon completion of training in May 1939 he was posted to 24 Squadron at Hendon as a communications pilot, flying such aircraft as the Vega Gull, Anson, Proctor, Flamingo and DH 84 and DH 86. In effect he was a taxi pilot. All the same, a taste of war came during the French campaign when John regularly flew service pilots and senior commanders around

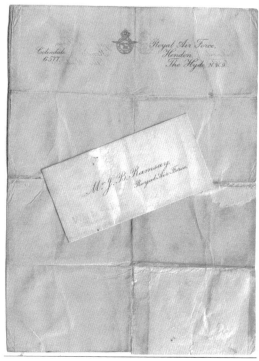

Helping to identify the pilot was an assortment of paperwork, including one of his RAF visiting cards.

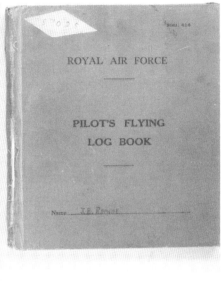

Until chance took a hand in matters all that the Ramsay family had to remember John by were his medals and flying log book. These are now in the author's collection.

continental Europe. It was during one of those taxi-flights that John met the RAF's 'ace' pilot, Fg Off 'Cobber' Kain when, on 25 May 1940 he flew him from Rouen-Boos to Gaye in France, flying in Vega Gull P1751. It was to be a momentous experience for John, but ultimately one that would cost him his life.

Impressed by the flamboyant and confident Kain, and buoyed up by his tales of derring-do as a fighter pilot John applied almost at once for a transfer to Fighter Command. Indeed, by 12 July, and with the shortages of fighter pilots stretching Fighter Command to its limits, he was posted to 7 Operational Training Unit at Hawarden for fighter pilot conversion. His first tentative flight on a Hurricane came on 15 July when he completed one hour and ten minutes on Hurricane L1825. By the time he was posted to 151 Squadron at North Weald on 30 July he had completed twenty-four hours and ten minutes on Hurricanes. For the month of August the squadron flew mostly convoy patrols or was ordered off on interceptions. For the most part his log book records: "No enemy aircraft seen," although he attacked formations of Dornier 17s over the Channel on 13 August.

On the 14th he witnessed Me109s in the distance but saw no action again until 18 August, the hardest fought day of the entire battle. He flew five times that day, each time in R4181, DX-C. On the fifth occasion he failed to return and his log book was stamped coldly in red ink: "DEATH PRESUMED". A little over a month had elapsed between John Ramsay's first tentative flight in a Hurricane and when he lost his life as a fighter pilot volunteering for front line service in the defence of Britain.

Closure. Joan Worth stands by her cousin John's grave-side with the officiating RAF chaplain. Joan was a formidable and dogged personality in the drive to get her much loved cousin a decent burial in accordance with his late mother's wishes. Without her it is unlikely that John would ever have been found or laid to rest.

When he was finally laid to rest at Brookwood Military Cemetery on 25 October 1983, Joan Worth was able to lay her wreath at his grave. On its card she had written:

"In affectionate memory of our dearest John who disappeared so long ago and who gave his life freely for us all. One of the few and one of the best."

CHAPTER 9
Finding Cock-Sparrow

IKE ANY schoolboy of the period, Frederick Prebble's priority once an aircraft was reported down was to cycle furiously to the scene. It mattered not whether the machine was one of ours or one of theirs...the name of the game was to get there before the police, the wardens or the army. Indeed, to get there before the rest of the local harum-scarum youngsters! At stake were the best souvenirs. Bits of perspex or spent bullets were all very well but more exciting pieces like guns or propeller blades earned the finder a fair degree of 'kudos' amongst his peers.

Thus when a Hurricane plunged into the ground by an orchard on the outskirts of Chelsfield during a fierce dogfight that had moved over from the direction of RAF Kenley in the afternoon of Sunday 1 September 1940, Fred Prebble was determined he would have the pick of the pickings. Dumping his bicycle in the hedge at Warren Lane he scampered over to where the plane had obviously fallen.

Wisps of smoke issued from a gash in the soil and debris was scattered around the loosened and blackened earth. In the naivety of his youthful enthusiasm, the search for souvenirs transcended any thought or consideration of what might have become of the pilot. As he scanned

Squadron Leader Peter Townsend, commanding officer of 85 Squadron during the Battle of Britain, called Sgt John Ellis the cock-sparrow. Much of his sparky personality is portrayed in this superb study of Ellis at Croydon shortly before his death. 'The Saint' emblem is painted onto his Mae West lifejacket.

the dismal scene Fred concluded that little of any value could be added to his collection from what remained here and he prepared to leave. Then, something caught his eye. A piece of white cloth fluttered in the breeze.

Protruding from a clod of earth thrown up on the edge of the crater was what for all the world looked like a handkerchief. Bending down, Fred went to pick it up but it wouldn't come. Tugging harder at the silky white material, he exposed several feet of cloth along with some plaited and woven lines. A parachute! Excitedly, Fred realised that he had himself a real trophy after all and pulling harder yet more of the canopy was uncovered, flapping loosely around his ankles. Clearly the whole parachute was not a viable proposition but luckily a panel appeared with the trademark of the Irvin Air Chute Company Ltd. Fred's schoolboy penknife was quickly put to good use and with a few deft strokes the panel was removed and in his pocket. Then it struck him. A parachute? If a parachute was here then so too must be its wearer. Without doubt a young man not much older than Fred had just died here. Horrified, Fred left the scene hurriedly but for years would think of this pilot and wonder who he might be. What had happened to him in that dogfight? Did anyone ever find him?

Three weeks after young Fred had collected his souvenir, an order was issued by 49 Maintenance Unit at RAF Faygate to the civilian contractors A V Nicholls & Co of Brighton. It read: "COLLECTION ORDER. Hurricane L2062. Chelsfield, NNW of Sevenoaks."

Arriving at Chelsfield the first port of call for the rather portly and Homburg-hatted Arthur Nicholls was the village constable. After checking Nicholls's credentials, the 'Bobby' was able to inform him that he knew of only one Hurricane on his patch. Close to the crossroads formed by Warren Lane and Court Road, the aircraft had come down in George Whitehead's field and had since been guarded by the Royal Artillery. At least, they had guarded what little was left. Once at the scene he made a quick assessment of what was needed for the job and forwarded his report to the CO of 49 MU, Sqn Ldr Goodman. It read:

"Hurricane L2062 – Chelsfield – NNW Sevenoaks
I located the site where the above aircraft had crashed as under:
    Court Road at the junction of the crossroads adjoining a road called Highways, (sic) Chelsfield.
    I interviewed the Officer Commanding 472 Bty RA's, on duty at a Listening Post in Highways, Chelsfield. He informed me that his men had been guarding the crashed aircraft by day but that there was no guard at night. He also informed me that the fuselage of the machine had been cleared by an RAF squad which he believed came from Uxbridge approximately two weeks ago. They informed him that they were returning for the engine later. Upon inspection I found that this machine had gone into the ground five or six feet. A propeller blade was visible embedded in the bottom of the crater. The engine was still in the ground. One or two pieces of broken fuselage remained.
    I have instructed a gang to clear the remainder of this wreckage, i.e. the engine etc on 23 September.
Signed: A V Nicholls"

The following day Nicholls's truck and two men arrived from Brighton. Meanwhile, Frederick and Ethel Ellis waited at their Cambridge home for news of their only child, John, missing since an air battle on 1 September. John's fiancé, Peggy Owen, was beside herself with worry as news if it came now could surely only be bad. But it never came. And that was worse.

John, like most fighter pilots of the period, was fatalistic in his outlook. He knew the odds and he knew they were stacked against him. Serving with 85 Squadron under Squadron Leader Peter Townsend and flying out of Croydon, he confided in Townsend that he knew how his end would come. "If I go it will be in the sea. One of my names is Mortimer. In other words, mort-i-mer; dead in the sea." All the same, Ellis and the other boys on 85 Sqn had to put such thoughts at the back of their minds and get on with things. To relax, Townsend's men spent much of their time listening to records on a wind up gramophone. 'Tuxedo Junction' was a special favourite;

John 'Hugh' Ellis is photographed here during one of his last home leaves with fiancé Peggy Owen. Later, Peggy's sister Grace told the author that Peggy had never found anyone else and had never married. "Her heart had died with Hugh," she said. This was a tragic but not uncommon outcome when boyfriends, fiancés or husbands failed to come home after being posted missing. Closure might well have enabled many of them to move on with their lives in some way.

> "....Don't you cry, don't ever shed a tear,
>   Don't you ever cry after I'm gone...."

But if John had fears for his safety then he kept them to himself – especially so far as Peggy was concerned. His Aunt Stella had sent him a lucky charm from Australia, a small boomerang that he wore round his neck. It would always ensure that he came back, he told Peggy. Then, on 13 August 1940, his great friend Peter Pryke was killed when his Wellington crashed on take-off from Bassingbourn. John attended the funeral at Cambridge a few days later and this was the last time his family and friends, including Peggy, ever saw him. Before he left for Croydon Peggy implored him to take care. Peter's funeral had underlined just how dangerous wartime flying could be. Not to worry, he told her. The boomerang would always get him back and, in any case, hadn't he another reason to look after himself? Hadn't Peggy's parents agreed to their marriage just as soon as he'd chalked up another Jerry?!

No sooner was John Ellis back on duty than Jerry had got him instead. Thankfully, though, the boomerang had worked. In a dogfight over Battle during the late afternoon of

29 August, John was shot down and had taken to his parachute as his Hurricane dived to destruction at Brigden Hill Farm, Ashburnham. It carried the code letter B. As an additional good-luck talisman he had chosen his aeroplane carefully – B for boomerang, apparently. Smashed to pieces, this Boomerang was certainly not coming back. The rest of the squadron, too, had fared badly. Sgt Walker-Smith had baled out wounded not far away at Etchingham and Sgt Booth had managed to just scrape home after a hairy dogfight off Eastbourne.

On the credit side, Booth had hit and damaged a Me109 which had had to crash land near Pevensey Chain-Home Radar Station whilst Peter Townsend had sent another diving into the ground at nearby Hooe. Shaken but unharmed, John Ellis had to get back to Croydon. He didn't want any worrying messages sent to his parents or Peggy. Incredibly, no transport could be found to take him and he had to make his way by bus and rail. It was a longish journey, and on the way he had time to reflect on his lucky escape. As he travelled he fingered his lucky boomerang beneath his shirt and found something that worried him. The tiny charm was broken having obviously bashed against something during his rapid evacuation of the Hurricane.

With the attrition rate amongst pilots at its height within RAF Fighter Command, John was lucky to be granted a few hours leave after his frightening episode on 29 August and made use of those precious moments visiting his aunt, uncle and cousins in nearby Mitcham. His cousin, Peter Mortimer, remembered that visit:

"He talked about baling out and said that he didn't have time to think. The first thing he knew he was out of the aircraft having had to leave it mighty quickly! He was concerned at what reception he would find on landing as the natives might be hostile. He was a bit put out that he had to return to Croydon by public transport, though.

"After this episode I remember his delight that he had either got or hoped to get a brand new Hurricane. I suppose the lowlier members of the squadron tended to get the oldest. Anyway, he said that he'd fly it over our home.

On Sunday 1 September, at about mid-morning, an aircraft roared low over our house. It was so low we all dropped to the floor – but then you ducked and asked afterwards in those days. Scrambling to my feet I saw a Hurricane disappear towards Tooting rocking its wings and then we realised it must have been him. Early that same evening his mother telephoned to say that he had been reported missing."

When John Ellis failed to return, the record on his personal casualty file held by the MOD was written up and an extract was provided to the author by the RAF Historical Branch as follows:

"It was initially suspected that he had crashed in the Kenley area where he was last seen in combat with Me109's. However, after six months when no trace of him or his aircraft was found the RAF authorities came to the conclusion that he had lost his life over the sea. His father, Mr F J Ellis, was informed of this on 4 April 1941 by the Officer Commanding 85 Squadron."

So, initially at least, it seemed as if John Ellis's prediction had come true and that he had lost

SUPPLEMENT TO REPORT DATED 22-9-40.

REPORT TO SQUADRON LEADER GOODMAN
R.A.F. DEPOT 24-9-40.

HURRICANE L 2062. Chelsfield, N.N.W. Sevenoaks.

My gang arrived on site of crash at Court Road Orchard, Chelsfield in the forenoon September 23rd. Commenced digging operations to remove embedded engine etc: They came across a "Flying" boot containing a foot; digging further they came across an unopened parachute, pulling on parachute exposed Pilot's body. Police were called to the site by gang supervisor, digging operations continued under surveillance of the Police, came across money (2/11½d), opened Pilot's pocket, found cigarette case also small wallet containing photograph of two ladies. All the above articles handed over to the police.
The Officers of the Police present were the local Constable stationed at Chelsfield and two Mobile Police Officers from Orpington. The Police took charge of the Pilot's remains. We cleared all remaining fuselage, one propellor blade and engine parts; filled in crater and left tidy.

Signed _____

This initially conflicting report relating to 'Hurricane L2062' at Chelsfield did not at first point to the crash site being Sgt John Ellis's Hurricane and left a big question mark hanging over this incident and the identity of its mystery pilot.

his life over the sea after all. Or had he? As things would turn out, the initial suspicions that Ellis had been shot down in the Kenley area were well founded.

When Arthur Nicholls's men returned to Chelsfield on 23 September, they were seasoned veterans of such tasks and what they were to find at Court Road Orchard was not unusual to them. The report filed by the salvage gang spares the reader none of the grim detail. Its inclusion on page 89 is justified as a vital piece of evidence in the case of John Ellis.

Unfortunately, the report gives no indication as to the identity of the pilot although one might presume that the aircraft number, L2062, would provide that link. Unfortunately it doesn't. Although L2062 was indeed lost in the area on 1 September 1940, it was actually a Hurricane of 79 Squadron and we know that it was being flown by Fg Off Brian Noble when shot down. However, Noble baled out to land in the water-filled Marley Sand & Gravel Pits at Riverhead and so we can be certain that the Court Road wreck was not his aeroplane. In comprehending how this confusion arose it is important to understand the system under which Nicholls operated. His instructions were based upon information collected by RAF crash inspectors who noted aircraft type, serial number and location of the wreck before passing the collection orders to A V Nicholls & Co via 49 MU at Faygate. Clearly the inspector had visited Noble's crash somewhere in the general vicinity and noted the serial number. When Nicolls then visited the local policeman he was directed to the only Hurricane he knew about – in Court Road. However, it was *not* L2062.

Local reports clearly indicate that on 1 September 1940, and at around 2.10pm, an aeroplane crashed at the Court Road site, with the 8 Group (London Region) ARP incident book recording merely:

"14.10hrs. High Exlosive bombs in orchard at Warren Road. Plane crashed in adjacent field. No damage to property."

Although further details are not recorded we do know from Nicholls's testimony that this crash certainly involved a fatality and by discounting the L2062 serial number it becomes possible, by the simple expedient of elimination, to conclude that the only likely contender for the crash is P2673, VY-E, flown by Sgt John Hugh Mortimer Ellis, 742068, of 85 Squadron. He was recorded as having no known grave and his name added to the Runnymede Memorial. It would be many years, however, before the case could be finally closed.

At some stage during the very early 1970s the Chelsfield crash came under investigation by the Halstead War Museum when enthusiasts Ken Anscombe and the late Gordon Anckorn apparently excavated the site. What they found there remains something of a mystery since the Halstead team was always very secretive in terms of publicising their finds. The case of the Chelsfield dig proved no exception. Indeed, during the production stages of the definitive book *Battle of Britain Then & Now* (edited by W G Ramsey), the museum refused to co-operate in any way with details of their extensive work in the sphere of wartime wreck investigations. However, it has been suggested by others present on this site dig that unspecified personal effects were found. In an effort to find out more for the Ellis family, the author spoke to Ken Anscombe on 31 October 1985 but was met with a firm

85 Squadron on a scramble at Croydon just a few days before Sgt Ellis died. Ellis is running on the left hand side in light coloured overalls.

denial. Mr Anscombe was adamant. Emphatically he told the author that he had no knowledge of any such excavation and could not help with any information.

Whatever the Halstead team did or did not find at Court Road, Chelsfield, during the 1970s is a matter that is eclipsed by one other over-riding question; what became of the body we know was found at the crash site by the salvage team in September 1940? Surely it must have been subject to formal identification and burial? It is here that the story takes another astonishing twist.

How and why the bodily remains recovered by Orpington Police in 1940 defied identification we shall probably never know but it seems very unlikely indeed that the clothing or effects held no clues whatsoever. Unfortunately, no police records exist for the district having long since been destroyed – although further research did reveal a possible clue. In the nearby cemetery of St Mary Cray there exists in Plot E128 a grave to an unknown airman of World War Two. No date is recorded on the headstone but the cemetery register shows the burial to have taken place on 5 October 1940 – just two weeks after the grim find of 23 September.

The possibility of a link is a strong one, although adding to the mystery is that yet another unknown airman was buried nearby – this time on 12 October 1940. Suggestions have since emerged that subsequent clearing up of the site after the Nicholls team left (and possibly some scavenging by passing gypsies) had resulted in the discovery of yet more remains, thus explaining the further interment on 12 October. No firm evidence exists, however, to link definitively either burial with Court Road, Chelsfield. Since neither set of bodily remains could have been buried without a death certificate, the local superintendent registrar kindly searched his indexes for the appropriate period. He reported that he was

91

Ministry of Defence, Air Force Board Secretariat,
Room 8239, Main Building, Whitehall, London SW1A 2HB

It shall be a condition of the grant of permission by the
Ministry of Defence that:

a.   the person to whom permission is granted shall
indemnify the Secretary of State against all claims
(including any action, proceedings, demand, costs,
charges and expenses) made against the Crown in
respect of injury (including death) to any person or
damage to any property (including consequential damage
or loss), and arising out of, or in any way connected
with, the recovery operations authorised by such grant;

b.   the Government shall not be responsible in any
way for any injury to the person to whom such permission
is granted or his death or damage to his property (including
consequential damage or loss) and that such person shall
be deemed to have voluntarily assumed the risks arising
in the recovery operations. It shall be the duty of such
person to draw to the attention of any persons assisting
in such recovery operations the existence of such risks

Attention is drawn to the desirability of persons obtaining permission
to undertake recovery operations to insure themselves adequately in
respect of the indemnity set out in a. above and the risks assumed
in paragraph b.

If you agree to the conditions as set out in paras a. & b. above
and in the Note of Guidance, please sign and return a copy of this
Annex as soon as possible.

....

A Hurricane, L2062, at Chelsfield.
    I agree to accept the conditions as set out in paragraphs
a. and b. above and in the Note of Guidance to Aircraft Recovery
Groups as issued by the Ministry of Defence.

Date: 30/5/80   Name: ....

                        Address: ....

                        ....

                        ....

Group Title: ..... WEALDEN AVIATION
             ARCHAEOLOGICAL GROUP ....

When the Wealden Aviation Archaeological Group applied for permission from the Ministry
of Defence to excavate this crash site during 1980, it was initially granted. Then, without
explanation, the MOD withdrew that permission and forbade any work at the crash site.
Despite being pressed for reasons for this *volte-face* the MOD declined to clarify why.
Whatever it was they knew about the Chelsfield site they were unwilling to say.

unable to find any linking entry. Any clues as to where these unknown airmen came from seemed to have been lost in the passage of almost seventy years and, thus far, have defied detection.

During the late 1970s, however, the then Wealden Aviation Archaeological Group decided that excavation of the mystery Court Road site would perhaps provide answers to many of these questions and obtained the landowner's permission to excavate. At this stage, and prior to legislative controls, the MOD requested that recovery groups seek formal permission from them before excavating. This was a purely voluntary exercise and not in any way an enforceable requirement. However, most recovery teams complied with the loose 'requirement' and, in this instance, the Wealden group sought and obtained MOD permission. The permission was based upon the then rather vague and mystifying assumption that this was Hurricane L2062 (as detailed in the Nicholls reports) although the purpose of the intended dig was to establish the true identity and hopefully to work out the history. Of course, from the available evidence of the Nicholls papers it seemed clear that the hitherto unidentified RAF pilot had been recovered and, presumably, he was named and buried somewhere. The question as to who he was and where he was buried had yet to be determined.

It was not until Mark Kirby excavated the crash site in 1992 that the mystery was finally solved and John Ellis was found. Here, Mark provides details at the crash site to Sgt Martin Gibbs the investigating police officer. John's niece stands on the right.

It was therefore a surprise for the Wealden group to then receive a further copy of the permission document from the MOD shortly before excavation was due to take place. It had been stridently crossed through in red, and marked in bold print: "PERMISSION WITHDRAWN 16.9.1980." Puzzled, the team sought an explanation as to this rather surprising turn of events but were simply told: "The MOD considers there are over-riding reasons why this site should not be subject to excavation." The saga of the Chelsfield Hurricane crash mystery was not over yet, though!

By the mid 1980s the author had established contact with members of the Ellis family and even tracked down Grace Owen, sister of John Ellis's late fiancé, Peggy Owen. Grace was fascinated by the tale of detective work that had now led to Chelsfield and, possibly, a grave (or graves) at St Mary Cray that might all be linked to John. Ultimately, Grace became convinced that the link was real and tangible and travelled down from her Cambridge home to visit Chelsfield and St Mary Cray. She wrote of that visit in July 1986:

"My sister Peggy's heart had died with Hugh (John) because she was never the same when she realised he was not coming back. I have now been to the places mentioned in your research dossier and feel the visit was really for Peggy. It was an emotional journey but one that I would not have missed. I am happy that his remains are probably in an English churchyard."

If Grace's mind had at least been put to rest, John's cousin Peter Mortimer was not content to let matters be. Enthusiast Mark Kirby, picking up the baton left behind by the Wealden group in 1980, was certain that excavation of the crash site would even yet unlock the mystery and enable John Ellis to have a named grave – either by providing some link to a St Mary Cray burial or, perhaps, by finding identifiable remains of either the aircraft or its pilot at the crash site.

Peter had already satisfied himself that the crash must certainly have involved his much-loved cousin and enthusiastically threw himself behind Mark Kirby who declared an intention to re-excavate the site. Peter Mortimer was clear that the exercise might reveal nothing, and equally clear that the dig might also uncover identifiable bodily remains of his cousin but he was adamant a dig should go ahead. In view of the MOD's 1980 stance, though, it was clear that no licence under the subsequently introduced 1986 legislation was ever likely to be granted but with the consent of the landowner and enthusiastic support of members of the Ellis family, Mark Kirby conducted an extensive unlicensed excavation at the crash site on Saturday 24 October 1992.

Present at the excavation, and at their specific request, were John Ellis's relatives who stood in the bitingly cold wind as they watched the final chapter of the mystery begin to unfold. Carefully and respectfully recovered from the crater were a quantity of bones, part of a Mae West life jacket and a flying glove intermingled with assorted items of aircraft wreckage. It was the wreckage that yielded the long elusive and all-important clue. Stamped into the corner of a portion of engine cowling was P2673 – the serial number of the Hurricane in which Sgt Ellis had been lost. At an inquest on 6 July 1993 HM Coroner formally identified the remains and told the Court: "I find that John Hugh Mortimer Ellis died on active service as a result of enemy action."

Despite the *prima-facie* case that might have perhaps existed against Mr Kirby for his actions in recovering John Ellis without an MOD licence, no action was taken against him. No doubt the active involvement of family members, the tacit support of local police officers for the recovery operation and the lack of any critical comments from the coroner played no small part in the MOD's failure to take any legal action. There was, however, a final twist to the whole saga when the police officer assigned to the case, Sgt Martin Gibbs, visited the owner of the Halstead War Museum to press for details as to what he had found in the 1970s. According to Mark Kirby the response was initially in the negative. Mark explains:

"Sgt Gibbs was insistent that whatever had been found in about 1970-ish be declared but was told there was nothing. Evidently Gibbs was not a man to give up, and pressed harder making it clear that this was a serious matter. His insistence worked and I am given to understand that a brass plate from the Rolls-Royce Merlin engine was then produced bearing the number 143834."

In 2007 Geoff Nutkins of the Shoreham Aircraft Museum organised the placement of this impressive stone memorial to Sgt Pilot John Ellis at the crash site in Chelsfield. From being lost and all but forgotten John's family, friends and former comrades-in-arms had finally been able to draw a line under a nagging mystery. His commemoration at Brookwood, and later at Chelsfield, ensures that his memory will endure – something that would not have happened in this way but for the intervention of researchers, enthusiasts and private individuals.

That number was highly significant. On the aircraft record card (AM Form 78) for Hurricane P2673 is logged its engine number – 143834. Had a clue linking Ellis to this site been in existence all along? Certainly it had been known about by someone since the early 1970s! Had Peggy Owen therefore died believing that her beloved John had gone to a watery grave? As her sister Grace put things in July 1993: "I only wish Hugh's parents and family, Peggy, and my parents had lived to know how near Hugh actually was."

Laid to rest with full military honours at Brookwood Military Cemetery on 1 October 1993, and in the presence of family members and Grace Owen, a wreath was placed on the grave from his former commanding officer, Peter Townsend. Of Ellis, Townsend wrote to the author from his home in France during 1993:

> "My memories of Hugh Ellis are of the fondest: his skill, his courage and his unfailing cheerfulness. I called him the cock-sparrow, so cheerful was he and such a marvellous pilot. Please convey to his relatives my deepest sorrow, relieved only by his being buried with military honours. I should like flowers at his funeral to be placed on his grave from me – flowers of blue, yellow and white. Blue for the sky, yellow for his hair and white for the flying overalls he invariably wore."

It had been a complicated search along a difficult trail, but the cock-sparrow had at last been found.

CHAPTER 10

Sgt Scott is No Longer Missing…

I N THE National Archives at Kew are the combat reports filed for the pilots of RAF Fighter Command during World War Two. Amongst them are the reports for 222 Squadron during the Battle of Britain. Mostly hand-written in pencil or ink on flimsy green pro-formas and signed by the pilots concerned, one of the 222 Squadron reports stands out from the others. It is typed on white paper, dated 27 September 1940 and signed by Plt Off S P S Raymond, Intelligence Officer. The body of the report reads:

> "This pilot, Sgt Scott, was missing on the patrol following this engagement without having time to write a report. He stated that at about 15,000ft he encountered an Me 109 and carried out a stern attack at 250 yards in one long burst. The enemy aircraft immediately dived and Sgt Scott followed it down and observed it crash in what appeared to be the playground of a school in Maidstone."

As Raymond's report intimates, Sgt Ernest Scott failed to return from a patrol later that same day.

Just a boy. Sgt Pilot Ernest Scott poses for a formal portrait in his RAF uniform. This same photograph was centrepiece in a shrine created at his Mansfield home by Ernest's grieving mother. Fresh flowers along with birthday cards and Christmas cards were regularly placed in front of the picture. Sadly, the Air Ministry had the evidence all along that would have pinpointed exactly where her son had been shot down.

Initially an RAF fitter, Ernest Scott is pictured here working on the engine of a Handley Page Heyford.

It was lunchtime at RAF Hornchurch in Essex, but on Friday 27 September 1940 Sgt Ernest Scott did not much feel like eating. Having just returned from the first patrol of the day, he was far too tense and too wound up as he waited for the next 'flap'. Besides, one of 222 Squadron's other sergeant pilots, Reg Gretton, had failed to come back from that earlier desperate combat over Kent and the Thames Estuary. It had made him feel sick, not hungry. To even the score, though, Ernest Scott had accounted for one Messerschmitt and sat excitedly describing the battle to 'Spy', the squadron intelligence officer. Plt Off Raymond listened and made a few brief notes about what Scott had told him, leaving Ernest with the parting shot: "Bang in a combat report, there's a good chap!" Skipping lunch, Ernest sat at dispersal and waited…waited for that dreaded telephone to ring with orders for the next shout of scramble! To take his mind off the tedium and to ease the nervous tension, Ernest took out one of the pale green combat report forms and started to scribble. Under General Report he wrote:

"I was leading Yellow Section when we saw a formation of 15-20 bombers with 20-30 Me 109's in the rear and slightly above. When they saw us they immediately broke up and scattered. I squirted a Me 109 which had a yellow nose and yellow tail plane and was flying at 15,000ft approximately.

I closed to 250 yards and opened fire in a long burst. I followed him down still firing. The Me 109 was definitely out of control and no doubt the pilot was killed. Still following it down in practically a vertical dive, I decided to pull out of the dive at about 4,000ft in order to prevent crashing myself and saw him crash on the out-skirts of Maidstone in what appeared to be a school playground.

Signed: E Scott."

Sgt Pilot Ernest Scott of 222 Squadron poses with a Spitfire at Hornchurch during the summer of 1940. The aeroplane is actually the commanding officer's machine, denoted by the squadron leader's pennant ahead of the cockpit. Noteworthy is the worn and weathered look of this Spitfire, splattered with oil and mud and somewhat scratched and battered.

Folding the report up, he pushed it into his flying map and tucked the map into the top of his flying boot. He would hand it in to Spy later. It could wait. Besides, before the day was out there would most likely be other combat reports to hand in. Indeed, by mid afternoon the squadron was off again – scrambled over Kent to meet further raids. Sgt Ernest Scott did not return.

Over the village of Hollingbourne, at around tea time, Ernest Scott's Spitfire drifted into the yellow ring of light which centred on the Revi gun sight of Major Werner Mölders's Me 109. In an instant, bullets and cannon shells had ripped into Spitfire P9364. The aeroplane immediately rolled over and then at full throttle screamed vertically into an orchard at Greenway Court, Hollingbourne. For Mölders, the flash of flame on the green countryside below confirmed another victory. Kill number forty-one could now be notched up on his rudder.

On the ground at Hollingbourne two sailors home on shore leave, Jim Humphries and Bill Smith, dashed to the scene. All they found was a hole in the ground surrounded by a few damaged fruit trees. There was simply nothing really to indicate that an aeroplane had crashed there. "It was unbelievable," recalled Jim. "All we could see was a crater in the ground. The plane had disappeared completely, dragging the soil back down on top of it. All I saw on the edge of the crater was a leather glove of the type pilots wore. As far as I recall there were only four people present. Ourselves, the farmer and the tin-hatted village Bobby. Nobody spoke. We were all too stunned."

Meanwhile, local reports were filed on the incident and the archives at the Kent County Records Office in Maidstone provide us with a vital linking clue to date and time the episode. In the war diary is noted the following:

"16.45hrs. Hollingbourne Head Warden reports at about 1600hrs a Spitfire crashed in an orchard. The owner is Mr Mark Whittaker of Greenway Court, Hollingbourne. It is believed pilot crashed with his machine. Slight damage to one tree."

Back at Hornchurch, Sgt Scott's failure to return was met with sadness. He was a much liked squadron member and a very experienced pilot and so his loss would be keenly felt. It would be more keenly felt, of course, back at his Mansfield home. His mother was never able to fully accept her son's disappearance, as Ernest's brother Albert was later to explain:

"In February 1941 the Air Ministry wrote to mother in a follow-up to the original telegram telling us that he was missing. The letter said that it was presumed Ernest had crashed into the sea and there was no hope of his recovery. In fact, that last information did give mother some hope. False hope, as it turned out. She always said that it was possible Ernest had been rescued from the sea by the Germans

Major Werner Mölders, the leading German air ace, was almost certainly responsible for shooting down Sgt Ernest Scott. Here he is featured on the front cover of a French language edition of the German magazine *Signal*. Sgt Scott became the major's forty-first victim. The tally for this particular kill on the rudder of his Messerschmitt 109 can just be seen over his left shoulder, and is dated 27 September.

and so for thirty years after her son went missing birthday cards and flowers were placed beneath his portrait which hung in the sitting room. Mother never gave up hope, and when she died on 22 May 1971, her final words were that she was going to join him."

After Jim Humphries and his friend had left the orchard at Greenway Court, the site was eventually visited some days later by 49 MU's crash inspector. Poking in the crater the RAF officer could tell it was a Spitfire and managed to find a piece of wreckage bearing the number P9364. Noting it down, he left. The report of the crash location for P9364 had been officially logged. The unfortunate thing was, as in many of these cases, that nobody ever made any link between Sgt Scott, P9364 and Greenway Court. Yet another RAF pilot would stay on the list of those unaccounted for at the war's end because of that not uncommon failing. Albert, Ernest Scott's brother, would ultimately have something to say about that when he wrote:

"Reports from the RAF recovery units, police, air raid wardens etc have proved without any doubt that the authorities have known all the time where these pilots lay! Yet nothing was ever done officially to extricate these brave young men at the time they crashed – and nobody has done anything officially since. But why has it been left to private groups and individuals to do the work on a voluntary basis in their spare time? We should be demanding that the Government should order the Ministry of Defence to recover these pilots once and for all."

In the case of his brother it would ultimately be those authorities who did recover him. He was not to know that when he wrote those words.

Again, it would be the activities of the private groups and individuals to whom Albert had referred who would finally be the catalyst for solving the question that had hung for so long over the Scott family about the fate of their Ernest. Despite the fact that many of the tales of detective work that surround these cases of missing airmen are complicated and complex, the case of Ernest Scott was deceptively simple.

In the public domain were RAF records that put Sgt Scott as being lost in Spitfire P9364 on 27 September 1940. In the same archive source were other RAF records that placed Spitfire P9364 on the ground at Hollingbourne. Kent County archives, meanwhile, confirmed that a Spitfire aircraft, with its pilot believed to be on board, was down at Greenway Court, Hollingbourne, on the date and time that corresponded exactly to the loss of Sgt Scott. Moving on one stage further, it was known that Sgt Scott hailed from Mansfield, Nottinghamshire, and the simple insertion of an appeal for relatives to come forward in the local newspapers resulted in brother Albert and sister Renee being traced.

With the family found, and Albert and Renee clearly anxious that no effort be spared to find Ernest, local enthusiasts Mark Kirby and Malcolm Pettit were not slow in approaching the landowner at Greenway Court, Hugh Batchelor, during the autumn of 1990. They were prepared to ride rough-shod over authority and to side step the issue of obtaining the MOD licence for recovery that the 1986 Protection of Military Remains Act now required. In any event, if confronted with the historical facts of the case then the MOD would certainly adhere to their firmly held policy and simply refuse a licence. If it meant bringing Ernest home then the means to the end was justified so long as Mr Batchelor would co-operate. But he emphatically refused to. Nobody could come onto his land to recover the Spitfire no matter who they were. With heavy hearts, Mark and Malcolm conveyed the bad news to brother Albert but wondered if a visit to Mr Batchelor by Albert and a face-to-face meeting with him might open the door? Albert readily agreed, but what happened next was the start of a roller-coaster of emotions of almost epic proportions. It almost becomes tedious to say it, but once again a sequence of events was about to unfold that utterly defies belief.

Intending to door-step Mr Batchelor with a photograph of his lost brother, an elderly Albert was at first disappointed to find Hugh Batchelor was out and he met instead Hugh's son, Richard. Amenable to the idea, and warming to Albert's poignant tale of loss, Richard

Evidence that Sgt Ernest Scott had at last been found was provided when the RAF excavated the crash site in 1990 and found this diary carrying his name.

told Mark and Malcolm that they could start work right away and a mechanical excavator was instantly booked to start work the following day, Saturday 17 November 1990. As they left Holligbourne, the pair drove Albert past the field where his brother had been lost. Later, Albert would write: "It was at this point that I vowed that my dear brother would be got out of that field and buried with the dignity and honour that a hero deserves." However, by later that same evening it became clear that it would be a much longer wait than had been anticipated following the meeting with Richard Batchelor, for by the time Mark and Malcolm had returned home a telephone message was waiting for them from Hugh Batchelor. He had rescinded his son's earlier permission to dig....and in spectacularly forceful terms. "Anyone who comes onto my land will face me and my shotgun!" was Hugh's final word on the matter. Albert was devastated. Again, his writings at the time summed up how he felt: "My mind was in a whirl from this bizarre affair. Could this all be true? Surely it's just a nightmare and I'll wake up from all this! Things didn't happen like this in real life, but then apparently they did. They were happening to me. I tried to gather my thoughts but blurted out 'Let me go there with you tomorrow, and if Batchelor uses that shotgun there will be two dead brothers together on his land!'"

It was set to get worse. Cruelly, the Batchelors changed their minds and relented – telephoning to say that work could start after all on Tuesday 20 November but, almost true to form, they changed their minds back again just the previous evening. Albert and Renee had had enough. More than enough. No was not an answer they were going to take and very soon letters were off to the Queen, Prince Charles and local MPs. A reply from Clarence House on behalf of Prince Charles on 30 November 1990 made it clear that His Royal Highness was concerned about the matter and that some sort of action would be taken. And indeed it was!

Over the weekend of 15/16 December 1990, a team from the RAF's Aircraft Salvage & Transportation Flight at RAF Abingdon set to work at Greenway Court. In a very short space of time they had recovered most of the wreckage of Spitfire P9364 along with its unfortunate occupant. Indeed, by late afternoon on the 15th Albert received a knock at his front door to find a police sergeant standing there with a message, and a telephone number, asking that he should at once 'phone a Squadron Leader Murphy. On making the call Albert was delighted to be told: "I have some good news for you. We have found your brother!" Ernest, who had been missing for fifty years, had been positively identified by a still legible diary in his tunic pocket. Tucked into a flying boot was a map of London and South East England with Ernest's un-submitted combat report neatly folded inside.

Although we can be sure that Sgt Scott fell victim to the Luftwaffe 'ace' Major Werner Mölders, we are spared the detail of knowing how, exactly, poor Ernest lost his life. One can only hope that the end was sudden. That he didn't die trapped inside a stricken aeroplane or, wounded, struggle helplessly to escape. All we know is the stark detail of that engagement as recorded for 222 Squadron in the RAF Hornchurch operations record book:

> "The third enemy attack *(of the day)* took place at 15 00hrs. Our squadrons left the ground late and sighted the enemy before they had gained sufficient height. Number 222 Squadron were attacked by Me 109's and lost Sgt Scott without themselves firing their guns."

If Sgt Scott had died that afternoon without firing his guns, we should at least look at his achievements and prowess as a fighter pilot up until the point of his untimely death. Assembled by the RAF Air Historical Branch for the Scott family in 1990, the following list of combat claims was put forward:

Dornier 17	– damaged	– 2 September 1940
Dornier 17	– destroyed	– 3 September 1940
Messerschmitt 109	– destroyed	– 3 September 1940
Messerschmitt 110	– destroyed	– 7 September 1940
Messerschmitt 109	– damaged	– 9 September 1940
Messerschmitt 109	– damaged	– 9 September 1940
Heinkel 111	– shared destroyed	– 11 September 1940
Heinkel 111	– shared destroyed	– 11 September 1940
Messerschmitt 109	– destroyed	– 27 September 1940

It is a not unimpressive tally, and given that the criteria set for the establishment of a fighter pilot as an ace is a total of five confirmed kills, then it will be seen that this is achieved by inclusion of the shared claims. Setting aside any post-war confirmation (or otherwise!) of this tally, it is only fitting that Ernest Scott's achievement is duly recognised here.

With the long overdue discovery of Ernest Scott at last expedited, it only remained for the RAF finally to bury one of its own. Beforehand, though, it fell to Wing Commander David Smale to write to Albert and Renee on behalf of the Ministry of Defence. In his letter of 13 December 1990, Smale set out to attempt to explain why Sgt Scott had been missing and why the family had been led to believe that he had fallen in the sea:

"At this late stage I can only hazard a guess that this lack of information was due to the constantly changing and sometimes confused conditions at the time which led the Casualty Office to conclude that Ernest's aircraft had crashed into the sea. Hence the explanation which was given to your mother in the Air Ministry's letter of 28 February 1941."

Of course, the fact of the matter was that the Air Ministry certainly had all the information it needed to explain exactly what had happened to Sgt Scott and had held this data all along. It was just that nobody had put the various reports and pieces of information together. Going on with his letter, Wing Commander Smale explained:

"However, the strongest evidence to emerge during our research to suggest that Ernest's aircraft had crashed at Greenway Court Farm comes from the records of 49 Maintenance Unit, Faygate; at the time this unit was tasked with the salvage of all crashed aircraft in the Kent area. The records show Spitfire P9364 as being in the Hollingbourne district but there is no confirmation that the wreckage was recovered."

As events just two days after the date of David Smale's letter would confirm, the wreckage of P9364 had certainly never been recovered. The records were correct – although, of course, all of this information had long been determined by amateur researchers and historians anyway. Finally, Wing Commander Smale offered a belated apology, of sorts, to the Scott family:

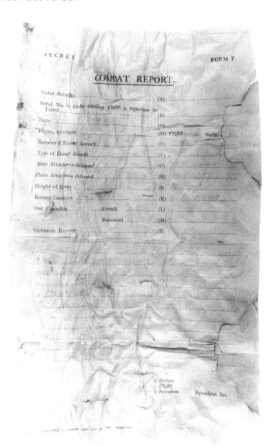

"Frankly, I am saddened to discover that the clues as to the aircraft's whereabouts were not investigated at the time of the crash or followed up at a later stage."

It was the closest anyone within the MOD had ever come to recognising that the policy adopted in the 1940s in respect of these missing casualties, and rigidly held on to in successive years, might in some way be flawed. It had taken action by private researchers, pressure by family members and intervention by a member of the royal family to bring Sgt Scott home. This finally happened on 1 February 1991. In a departure from the usual convention adopted in the case of most other post-war

Other documents were also found in 1990 that identified Ernest Scott – including this completed combat report for an action earlier that same day, 27 September 1940.

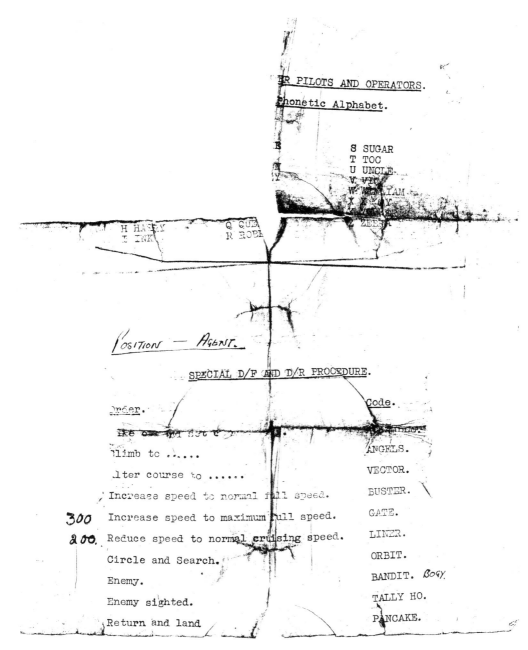

Another document revealed in the long-buried cockpit of Sgt Scott's Spitfire was this typed phonetic alphabet and a list of now iconic RAF code words – words like scramble, angels, buster, bandit and tally-ho.

casualty discoveries in the UK, he would not be buried at Brookwood Military Cemetery. Instead, the ceremony was held at RAF Manston and he was finally laid to rest in the nearby cemetery of St John's, Margate. Whilst members of the same service were, at that very moment, flying and dying during the prosecution of the first Gulf War the funeral address was delivered by the station commander of RAF Manston. He concluded his moving address with the valediction:

"Sgt Scott did not want or seek to lose his life. But he was willing to risk it for things that matter. It was taken from him at the threshold of achievement. But in his short span he did more than most of us. It is our honour to recognise that today. Sgt Pilot Ernest Scott is no longer missing."

Final respects. Veterans of 222 Squadron and the Battle of Britain gathered at Manston to say farewell to 'Scotty', including Wing Commander Ivor Cosby on the left.

CHAPTER 11 Mistaken Identity

Michael Doulton was reckoned to be the tallest RAF pilot in service and he is easily picked out here in the centre of the back row of this 1933 photograph of his pre-war auxiliary air force squadron, No.604 'County of Middlesex' Squadron, during its summer camp at Tangmere.

DURING THE lunch-time period on 31 August 1940, Fg Off Michael Doulton sat at readiness in the heat of his cockpit reading a novel – *The Keeper of The Bees* by Gene Stratton-Porter. He was probably starting to feel uncomfortable in the oppressive heat kitted out in the pre-war black flying overalls he still habitually wore. Suddenly, 601 Squadron (the so-called 'Millionaires' Squadron) were called to go. Michael Doulton stuffed his unfinished book into the map box. He would finish reading it on his up-coming leave, he thought. Strapping himself in he pulled on his helmet and goggles and

107

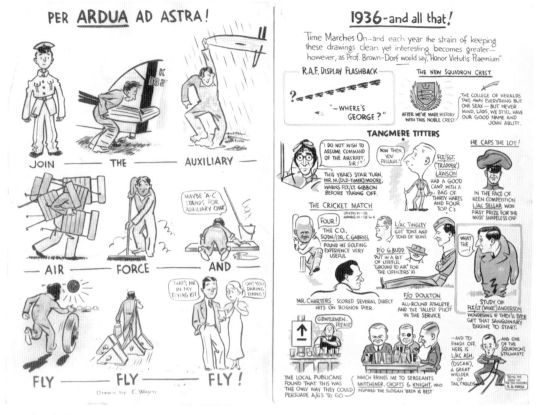

Michael's height was also emphasised in this squadron caricature montage by the cartoonist Wren.

started up. The cool blast of a slipstream from the spinning propeller was momentarily refreshing before he slammed shut the canopy. Only this trip to do and then he had some leave. In fact, he should have already left by now for Chichester where his young American wife Carol, pregnant with their first child, was waiting for him at their cottage near RAF Tangmere where earlier he had been based. However, he was content to do just one more sortie to make up the numbers. Then he'd be off for home.

By 13.00hrs the twelve Hurricanes of 601 Squadron were bounding across the field at RAF Debden and airborne for the Colchester area where they were to patrol at 15,000ft. By 13.30 the squadron had been vectored onto a course taking them over Tilbury and the Thames Estuary and had climbed to 10,000ft. Almost at once a large mass of enemy aircraft were sighted coming directly from the east and comprising two groups of Dornier 17s in tight formation escorted above and behind by large gaggles of Me 109s. Climbing and turning in from the south, 601 Squadron readied to attack the formation but, before they could do so, were engaged by the enemy fighters. A confused dogfight ensued and although we know the detail of some of the individual combats that the 601 Squadron pilots had, it does not help us any in understanding what happened to Michael Doulton. Suffice to say that he was last witnessed entering the fray and was then not seen again. When the head-count was taken back at Debden, Doulton was missing. Sergeants Taylor and Woolley had been shot down and had baled out, as had Plt Off H T Gilbert. But of Doulton there was simply no trace.

Back at their cottage, a devastated Carol tried to take in the news and was comforted by fellow pilots and respective wives and girlfriends. Within a few weeks it was clear that Michael was not coming back. Pragmatic, Carol did not cling to any forlorn hopes about his being rescued by boats or being a prisoner of war. She already considered herself a widow. With nothing to keep her in England, and no family to support her here, Carol made the dangerous journey back to the USA where giving birth to her child in the bosom of family and friends was clearly the best option. Anyway, it was away from the bombs and the danger and all the privations of war. With a heavy heart, Carol left England knowing that she would never see Michael again. The prospect that he would ever be found seemed a remote one.

When 601 Squadron had gone into battle over the Thames Estuary on that August afternoon it was not alone. Joining in the combat were other RAF fighters – included amongst them the Hurricanes of 310 (Czechoslovak) Squadron and the Spitfires of 603 Squadron. With such a large number of aircraft turning and wheeling in such a small space of sky, the dogfighting

Michael Doulton pictured with his young American wife, Carol.

and the individual scraps and skirmishing were as confused as any aerial battle ever could be. Somewhere amongst the diving, turning, wheeling and soaring fighters Michael Doulton's Hurricane had plunged away earthwards, unseen. So too had the 310 Squadron Hurricane of Plt Off Jaroslav Sterbacek. Of 310 Squadron, Plt Off Kredba was forced to bale out and Pilot Officers Fechtner and Maly returned to their Duxford base with damaged aeroplanes. Like Doulton, Sterbacek had simply vanished.

Fast-forwarding to 13 August 1978 we find the crash site of a Hurricane on Wennington Marshes, near Romford, Essex, coming under investigation by the Essex Historical Aircraft Society. Team member Robin Hill takes up the story:

"In the Essex Records Office the original report of a crash at Wennington stated not only the date, time and location but also, somewhat surprisingly, contained the rather cryptic and intriguing statement 'markings visible' in the description of the event. I have often wondered if it should have read 'markings invisible' with the mistake being explained as a transcription error when the message was telephoned in to the reporting centre.

Either way, if markings were visible it frustratingly didn't tell us what they were! Anyway, a conclusion was, at some point, somehow reached that this was where Jaroslav Sterbacek had crashed as the date and time corresponded to his loss and just before our eventual excavation of the site we were as a society made aware of a locally held belief that this site was actually a war-grave.

"As to the dig itself, well, when we first found the site it was a flooded depression some eighteen inches deep. We only used an ordinary JCB which turned out to be completely inadequate for the task in hand. I think it spent more time digging itself out than digging in the hole and we had to 'appropriate' a couple of railway sleepers to actually get the digging machine out. Throughout the excavation the sides repeatedly caved in and in the end we struggled down to a depth of twelve to fourteen feet. At the bottom was an oily black stain, and all we recovered was a section of radiator, the bottom of the sliding canopy, a piece of centre section structure, smashed up bits of engine casing and six of the eight Browning machine guns. We found no major engine components, no substantial fuselage wreckage and no trace of the cockpit."

In fact, nothing had emerged from the Essex group's dig to point positively to its identity as Hurricane P3159 – the aircraft in which Sterbacek had been lost. By 1980, however, and the publication of *Battle of Britain Then & Now* the Wennington crash had 'become' Jaroslav Sterbacek's aircraft. Perhaps it was an entirely reasonable assessment as the Essex group excavators had been emphatic about its identity. On their part it had been a dangerous conclusion to make. In reality, there was not a shred of any substantive evidence that pointed to Sterbacek above Doulton – neither in historical documents nor amongst the meagre finds from the 1978 excavation.

Speaking to the author in 2008, Robin Hill conceded that point wholeheartedly, adding the observation that if a statement of historical detail is quoted often enough it becomes an established historical fact – even if it is not. Indeed, and although he did not say how he knew *(and this was long before the publication of* Battle of Britain Then & Now*!)* Wennington resident John Hall was absolutely adamant that local knowledge had established the pilot to be Sterbacek. Retired War Reserve Special Constable George Matthews was also convinced, as he wrote in 1979: "The pilot had no chance to escape and had died in his 'plane. He was Polish, I understood at the time." Polish? Czech? It is easy now, with the benefit of hindsight, to see how a picture was built up and the 'facts' became firmly established in the way Robin Hill had so succinctly put it. Its inclusion as fact in published sources merely cemented its veracity. The conclusions drawn would come back to haunt all of those who were eventually to be involved in a much later part of the Wennington Hurricane saga.

It was not until 1984 that the site again came under further investigation, this time when Dave Smith of the Medway Aviation Research Group took matters up. His colleague and fellow researcher, the late Alan Brown, had made contact with the brother of Jaroslav Sterbacek, Oldrich, still living in what was then Czechoslovakia. Oldrich was both fascinated and moved to learn of the researches surrounding his late brother and realised from discussions with Alan that he must still be in the wreck of his Hurricane. Oldrich, and other family members, were desperate to have the wreck recovered so that their brother could be

Flying Officer Michael Doulton remained missing until April 1984 when he was found in the wreck of his Hurricane on an army rifle range at Wennington Marsh in Essex. The tricky recovery operation was led by Dave Smith of the Medway Aviation Society.

properly laid to rest. Alan explained that it would be difficult, but with the right equipment it might yet be possible. The interest of the Sterbacek family coincided, as it so happened, with Dave Smith's revival of interest in the crash site and Dave was willing to proceed with a recovery subject to the permission of the MOD.

In this instance the MOD were also the landowners as the site was part of an army firing range. However, there were yet other complications to consider; what of the question of the occupant of the aeroplane? And what evidence was there to support the notion that this was indeed Sterbacek's aeroplane? David proceeded with understandable caution and had to weigh up all the evidence available to him. In this context, Robin Hill was consulted again but could add little or nothing – either way – in respect of the pilot's identity.

Despite the school of thought that still firmly held this to be Sterbacek's crash site, Robin would concede that there simply was no evidence. In actual fact, no less than six Hurricanes were shot down in this immediate vicinity in that particular combat. In reality, it could be any of them although only two losses (Sterbacek and Doulton) involved casualties who were still unaccounted for. The others, one way or another, had been detailed in 1940 even if the location of their respective crash sites was a little uncertain now, in 1984. Undeterred, David ploughed on with his research and eventually came to the conclusion that Doulton had probably crashed into the sea or Thames Estuary and that a very strong contender for the pilot of the Wennington crash was Pilot Officer Miroslav Kredba of 310 Squadron who had baled out. Witnesses Dave spoke to talked about a parachute and it was thought that the pilot was Polish. Either way, and whomsoever the pilot might have been, the 1984 rules did not require much detail to be submitted to the MOD for what was then an unenforceable and nominal permission that the ministry then asked excavators to seek. That said, tying the site to Sterbacek when seeking MOD authority would have certainly resulted in a refusal and Dave wished to toe the line as far as possible.

In any event, reasoned Dave, the MOD had at their disposal all of the official casualty files on all of those lost that day. Not only that, but it was known that the MOD branch then involved in licence issue had in their office the *Battle of Britain Then & Now* book that was apparently often used as an initial reference check by them. Anyone checking the entry for Kredba would see printed boldy above, below and alongside that very entry the details about Sterbacek's loss along with photos and details appertaining to the 1978 dig at the Wennington location. An obvious link thereby existed to the site with the request for permission that was now being filed. Not only that, but the site itself *belonged* to the MOD and surely the managing agency for the army would need to be satisfied, too?

Ultimately, permission was granted to excavate the site by the MOD in its capacity as both landowner and the overseeing authority. From Dave Smith's perspective, though, the likelihood that this might be Sterbacek's aeroplane was something that still needed to be carefully considered although there was the comfort that the family wanted recovery undertaken. Backing up their desire, Alan Brown had secured a written authority from Oldrich and other close family members which had been signed by them and dated 12 March 1984. Alan handed the authority to Dave Smith, although Dave expressed his fears lest the pilot wasn't Sterbacek after all. Best, he considered, to proceed with caution and not to tell the Sterbacek family of the immediate plans to excavate lest their hopes be dashed. As things would shortly turn out, Dave's caution about the pilot's identity and his reticence in not telling the Sterbacek family of the plans already in train were both well placed. On 27 April 1984, Dave Smith assembled his team and finally excavated the crash site at Wennington. In the cockpit they found the remains of a pilot. It wasn't Sterbacek.

Dave's team had very quickly located the main aircraft constructor's plate on which, very clearly, was stamped the serial number of this particular Hurricane – R4215. Sterbacek had been lost in P3159. The pilot who had failed to return in Hurricane R4215 on 31 August 1940 was Fg Off Michael Duke Doulton. The discovery of that data plate on site in April 1984 immediately told the recovery team who the pilot was and by the time the police had been called to the site they were able to pass this information to the coroner's team. Ultimately matters

When the remains of the pilot were uncovered they were initially suspected to be those of Jaroslav Sterbacek who had been shot down on 31 August 1940 in the same area to become the first Czech to die in RAF service.

The discovery of the aircraft maker's plate from a Gloster-built Hawker Hurricane revealed the serial number to be R4215 – the aeroplane in which Michael Doulton had been lost.

would now follow the proper channels through the respective authorities – the MOD and HM Coroner. Matters were now out of Dave Smith's hands. However, there were more twists yet to come.

The author had been part of Dave's team invited to the April 1984 recovery and ahead of any formal identification of Doulton, had been curious as to where the Doulton family might be. The CWGC register for the Runnymede Memorial gave him as the husband of Carol, of Vinehall in Sussex. This was a puzzle. Where on earth was Vinehall? No gazetteer showed a place of any such name – although it did ring a very big bell. Not far from the author's home stood Vinehall School near Robertsbridge in East Sussex. Could it be connected? The author duly telephoned the school and in one of those utterly remarkable coincidences that seem to follow many of these cases, the 'phone was answered by the school's ex-headmaster. It was a weekend (the day after the Wennington recovery, in fact) and Mr Richard Taylor just happened to be visiting the school.

In the tangled wreckage of the cockpit a portion of black pre-war flying overalls was found bearing the badge of 604 Squadron on the breast pocket. (see photograph on page 107) This had been Michael's peacetime squadron although he was serving with 601 Squadron when shot down and killed.

Richard was astonished when the reason for the call was explained. Himself an ex Spitfire pilot who had flown with 602 Squadron just after the Battle of Britain, he knew Michael Doulton's widow well. Now Carol Gilbart, she had been a teacher at Vinehall and was a close friend of Richard's who had also known Michael pre-war. Within the hour the author was sitting in Richard Taylor's lounge explaining the previous day's find at Wennington. Carefully, the scenario was explained and Richard took the view that Carol would ultimately be pleased that Michael had at last been discovered. However, he was concerned about her initial reaction and as she was again a widow he felt that she should not be alone when the MOD might send an RAF officer to knock on her door.

For the time being it was clearly not appropriate to tell her. The identity of the pilot was still subject to formal clarification. In any case, the author and Richard Taylor both reasoned that the MOD might anyway now have great difficulty in finding Carol. Not only had she re-married, but her Vinehall address might fox anyone trying to find the place – unless they happened to have a fairly intimate knowledge of that part of Sussex. By the time officials at the MOD were assessing the news about Doulton's discovery at their desks on the Monday morning, and before they had time to pull Fg Off Doulton's casualty file, Richard Taylor had telephoned them with news of Carol Gilbart's whereabouts with a request that any contact with her was channelled through him.

Back in Essex, the local coroner's officer PC Bob Goddard had taken charge of proceedings and it was not long before a positive identity had formally and officially been established. However, that was not before the local press had picked up the story of the discovery of the pilot's remains and had begun to run articles about the finds. At this stage, formal identification was still pending and so no details were released to the press by either Essex Police or by the coroner. For their part, Dave Smith's team were equally tight lipped about who the pilot was – although, of course, they now knew.

"A verray parfit gentil knight". After a quiet cremation service at Hastings, Michael's ashes were interred at Salehurst in East Sussex on 15 September 1984, Battle of Britain day. Visitors to the cemetery might well puzzle over the fact that Michael's date of death actually pre-dates by very many years the establishment of the cemetery in which he now lies! Events surrounding his discovery and eventual funeral and interment were shrouded in secrecy by the Ministry of Defence – largely to shield his widow, Carol, and to prevent any unwanted media interest with the family link to the Royal Doulton porcelain company. He was even cremated under the pseudonym of 'Martin Smith' to prevent snooping reporters making any connection.

At this stage, enter a member of the team who had previously been involved in the earlier unsuccessful excavation of the site by the Essex group in 1978. Probably well meaning, but without any knowledge at all as to what had subsequently come to light, the individual concerned contacted the press with news that he could certainly identify the pilot. It was Jaroslav Sterbacek, he told them. On 4 May 1984 the local *Thurrock Gazette* ran the story and "confirmed" the pilot's identity! Once again, another remarkable coincidence took place. This time it was an exceedingly unfortunate one.

Oldrich Sterbacek, anxious for news of what might be happening in the search for his late brother and knowing that something was going on, had decided to visit England to make his own enquiries. That he should visit Essex at that particular time was almost beyond belief. That he should then read the newspaper stories about his brother's discovery and "identification" was going one stage further than coincidence. Very soon he was knocking on PC Goddard's door wanting to know more. The unfortunate Bob Goddard, knowing full

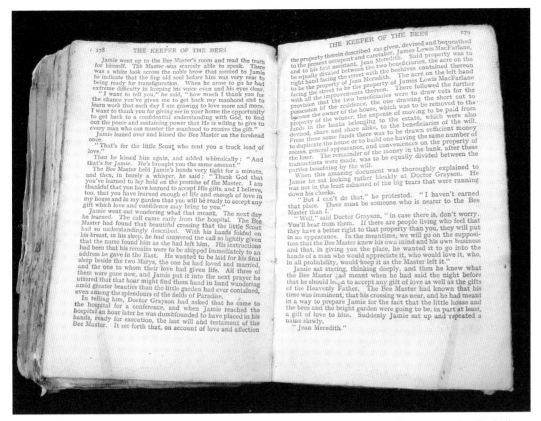

Before he had taken off on his fatal last flight, Michael had been reading a novel called *The Keeper of the Bees*. His book, still entirely legible, was found in the cockpit.

well that this was not Jaroslav Sterbacek's body, tried to explain the circumstances to an angry and distraught Oldrich who ultimately vented his displeasure with the MOD. No doubt his emotions were running high and he felt that he had been misled by everybody involved. It had certainly been unfortunate and unforgivable that he should have had his hopes raised and then so cruelly and comprehensively dashed by irresponsible reporting and by the exceedingly unwise and questionable actions of one who had tipped off the press about the pilot's apparent identity. The press should have known better; putting information like this into the public domain as 'fact' before formal identification had been announced and the family informed, broke all the rules of journalism.

Carol Gilbart, and her son Paul Doulton, were initially shocked by the discovery of Michael but in later years she was in contact with Dave Smith and confided to him that the find had ultimately comforted her. When Michael was eventually cremated at a very private ceremony in Hastings, the family and the MOD had gone to great pains to keep things very private. There was no military funeral with honours. No bands. No flag draped coffin. No press releases. It suited the MOD, too, that the case was kept so very low-key. After all, they must have been sensitive to the fact that the excavation had taken place on MOD land and, additionally, that its location and possible association with a missing pilot had been very well known. Indeed, all the details were plainly recorded in a published source that undoubtedly sat on an MOD desk. For her part, Carol also no doubt felt that she could not cope with the press attention that might ensue – not least of all because any likely press interest would be generated by the fact that Michael Doulton was of the Royal Doulton porcelain dynasty. Michael's ashes were eventually interred in the tiny burial ground at Salehurst in East Sussex under a CWGC headstone.

Carol Gilbart is now buried next to him. At the foot of Michael's headstone is carved:

"A verray parfit gentil knight"

Taken from Chaucer's *Canterbury Tales* *(Prologue 1:4:3)* it is an appropriate inscription given Michael Doulton's deep love of literature. That love of the written word emerged with him into the spring sunshine on Wennington marshes one April day in 1984 when his book *The Keeper of The Bees*, long overdue from RAF Tangmere's station library, tumbled out of the wreckage at the author's feet. With leaves fluttering in the breeze it poignantly fell open on the very last page Michael had read.

Jaroslav Sterbacek, meanwhile, is still missing.

And what of Jaroslav Sterbacek? After the debacle over events following the recovery at Wennington, a headstone bearing his name was erected in the Czechoslovak plot at Brookwood Cemetery leading to supposition that he had, after all, been found somewhere else. In fact, this standard pattern Czech headstone is merely a commemorative memorial. He is not buried here and has not yet been found.

CHAPTER 12

Blue One Still Missing…

WHEN AN excavation over the weekend of 28/29 July 2007 at Albion Parade, Gravesend, by a team of Royal Engineers and RAF personnel failed to find any trace of the Hurricane aircraft or of its pilot, Flt Sgt Eric Williams, lost there on 15 October 1940, it seemed that the mystery of this pilot's last resting place would endure. Indeed, that was how the situation was described on the official Ministry of Defence news website immediately after those July excavations. Subsequently, however, there were further developments enabling us to look anew into the sad yet fascinating saga of a still missing Battle of Britain pilot.

Since early September 1940, 46 Squadron had been operating from RAF Stapleford and had participated in the latter half of the Battle of Britain as part of 11 Group Fighter Command. Here, the squadron had taken many casualties along with the tally of victories they had notched up. By 15 October they were surely a tired and battle-weary unit, but still manfully participating in holding the line against the continuing Luftwaffe onslaught. At around 12.30hrs on that date, twelve Hurricanes took off from Stapleford for a patrol. Leading them was Flt Sgt Eric Williams and, although junior in rank to many other

Flight Sergeant Eric Edward Williams of 46 Squadron was shot down and killed at Barton's Timber Wharf in Gravesend on 15 October 1940 but never found. Although the RAF knew exactly where he had crashed the family were not informed. It was not until the author's research team contacted Eric's widow and daughter that they learned the truth – that his body was deep beneath the dirt floor of a Thames-side industrial unit.

Eric Williams had previously served as a Blenheim pilot on 29 Squadron before joining 46 Squadron to fly Hurricanes. He is seen here (on the right) with other 29 Squadron pilots. To his right is Bob Braham, later to become a famous night-fighter ace.

squadron pilots, he was arguably one of the most experienced amongst them – having been a fighter pilot since 2 September 1934. An additional factor in Eric's leadership of the squadron that day may well have been the almost transient nature of 46 Squadron COs around this time. On 6 October, the Commanding Officer, Squadron Leader J R MacLachlan, had been posted away with Squadron Leader A R Collins taking over. By 31 October he had been replaced by Squadron Leader L M Gaunce.

Between 12.57 and 13.08hrs on 15 October 1940, though, three Hurricanes had returned to Stapleford – Blue Two and Green Two with oxygen problems and Green Three with engine problems. Shortly before this, at 12.55hrs, Blue One (Flt Sgt E Williams) with the remainder of the squadron and flying at 15,000ft reported on the R/T that he had spotted twenty to thirty Me 109s milling overhead at 25,000ft. The squadron commenced to climb as rapidly as possible and were then vectored nine-zero. As the Hurricanes headed eastwards and climbed, the enemy aircraft above them were then able to position themselves between the squadron and the sun and delivered an astern attack from above and out of the sun. It was a classic fighter bounce. In this instance, the bouncers had been the Messerschmitt 109s of Adolf Galland's Jagdgeschwader 26, 'Schlageter'.

As the Messerschmitts tore unseen into the Hurricanes that were straining on their propellers to gain altitude, two pilots of I Gruppe and two pilots of II Gruppe each claimed a Hurricane as destroyed. Galland, the Geschwader Kommodore, claimed a 'Spitfire' in

Adolf Galland was involved in the dogfight when Williams was shot down. Here he shows Italian Air Force officers the victory tallies on the rudder of his Messerschmitt 109 immediately prior to the action in which Eric was shot down.

the same combat – the forty-sixth victory for this ever-rising star.

In the slashing attack by the Messerschmitts, Oblt Henrici and Uffz Scheidt got their sixth and third aerial victories respectively. Meanwhile, Hptm Adolph and Oblt Grawatsch downed their twelfth and second kills. Without doubt, their victims were the Hurricanes of 46 Squadron who JG 26 reported to have attacked in the Gillingham/London area. As for Galland, his claim for a Spitfire was in the Rochester/Gillingham area. However, no Spitfire losses that day match this time or location and so it is entirely possible that he, too, engaged the same group of Hurricanes but perhaps misidentified the type during the heat of battle. A not uncommon event.

As the Messerschmitts tore through the squadron, Pilot Officer Robert Reid (Green One) was startled to see tracer bullets from nowhere suddenly entering the cockpit of Blue Three and then tracers hitting Blue One (Eric Williams) with some effect. Almost immediately, a Me 109 appeared just fifty feet above him and to the left. Pulling up the nose of his Hurricane he got in a two second burst at the enemy, and saw bullets entering the cockpit and right across its wings causing the Messerschmitt to turn over emitting grey smoke and to spiral down out of control. Reid followed, down to 10,000ft, before pulling out. Red One (Fg Off Lefevre) saw what was believed to be the same Me 109 entering the clouds below him at 2,000 to 4,000ft, although due to the cloud conditions it was impossible to see the enemy crash but the estimated location was in the vicinity of Rochester and the Medway towns. In just a matter of seconds, the engagement was all over. 46 Squadron had been broken up and badly mauled, losing three Hurricanes and having one more damaged. Pilot Officer Gunning was dead, and Flight Sgt Williams was missing. Meanwhile, Sgt Gooderham had baled out with facial injuries, a bruised arm and a damaged knee.

(Note: although a 2007 MOD press release attributed the loss of Flt Sgt Williams directly to Adolf Galland, there is no absolutely definite evidence of this although Galland may possibly be the victor.)

Across the River Thames Pilot Officer P S Gunning (inset) of 46 Squadron was shot down and killed during the same engagement. His Hurricane fell into a quarry at Little Thurrock in Essex where its remains were photographed prior to removal by haulage contractors. The contrast in this photograph is unfortunate, but a wing with its roundel clearly rests against the quarry face. To the left, wreckage burns and sends up a pall of black smoke behind the first wagon and wreckage is scattered on the edge of the quarry to the right. Regrettably no ground-level photograph exists to help us position Eric Williams's crash site.

On the ground at Gravesend it was lunchtime, and Walter Holden was just about to leave his work at the timber depot of W R Barton & Sons Ltd in Albion Terrace when he heard the roar of a descending aircraft. Although he could not see it, he realized from the sound that it was headed towards either the River Thames or nearby Albion Parade where his firm's timber wharf was situated. The noise of the impact told him all he needed to know and he immediately rushed to the scene. By the time he arrived it was obvious something had happened but he was surprised to find the fire, police, ARP and ambulance services already there.

Making himself known, he was allowed into Barton's Wharf and found a gaping hole torn in the shed roof. No timber was stored there at the time, and in the soft dirt floor beneath the damaged roof was a large imprint with shreds of metal strewn around. Water, fuel and oil was bubbling and seeping into the crater. Of the pilot there was no trace, and those initially on the scene had no idea whether he had baled out or failed to escape from his aircraft.

Gradually, the facts were pieced together and it became clear that the pilot of this

Now demolished, these are the original timber storage sheds at Barton's Timber Wharf in Gravesend beneath which lies Eric Williams's Hurricane. Pictured from Albion Parade, the actual crash site is just inside the shed near the distantly parked car.

aircraft had not been accounted for. At first, there was some speculation that he may have fallen unseen and with an unopened parachute into the adjacent river – some half a mile wide at that point. Investigations at the site, though, soon revealed the grim truth when a Royal Engineer party dug down into the crater and recovered part of a flight sergeant's sleeve badge. There was only one contender; Flight Sergeant Eric Williams.

Upon Eric's failure to return to Stapleford that afternoon after Pilot Officer Reid had seen the tracer bullets smashing into the Hurricane, enquiries were immediately made by the squadron adjutant as to what had become of him. Police, hospitals, the observer corps, military units and other RAF stations in the region were canvassed. No information was forthcoming, although the report of a Hurricane landing with combat damage at RAF Hawkinge gave some initial promise but turned out, instead, to be a Hurricane and pilot of 257 Squadron. With the other 46 Squadron losses accounted for, and the known circumstances of the Albion Wharf crash established, it was concluded that Eric Williams was missing in action. Accordingly, the standard terse air ministry telegram was sent to Eric's wife, Joan, notifying her that her husband was missing as the result of air operations. Eventually, after the passage of some months, his death was presumed. In fact, the RAF had already established with some clarity the location of his crash and, indeed, the place of his death. The 46 Squadron operations record book for 15 October 1940 was unambiguous on the matter:

"F/Sgt E Williams was missing from this patrol, but it was later confirmed that his machine had crashed near Gravesend and his death had occurred."

The casualty file for Eric Williams was equally clear, and enabled the RAF's Air Historical Branch to be able to confirm in the 1970s:

"The Hurricane aircraft (V6550) piloted by Flight Sergeant Williams was shot down at approximately 13.00hrs on 15 October 1940. The aircraft crashed onto a wharf, approximately one mile east of Gravesend Ferry Railway Station."

Unfortunately, Joan Williams wasn't told. All she then knew was that he was missing, presumed dead. Later, and almost to draw some kind of official line under it, his name was added to the RAF's Runnymede Memorial to airmen who are missing and who have no known grave. Indeed, there the matter may well have rested had it not been for research conducted by the author and his colleagues during the late 1970s and early 1980s.

With the upsurge of interest in researching the losses of Battle of Britain aircraft during that time it was inevitable that interest would, at some stage, focus on the Albion Wharf crash. Eye witness accounts like those of Walter Holden abounded from those who were there in Gravesend during 1940 and a certain amount of folklore and legend had developed – but it was well known that the aeroplane was still buried there, and with its pilot. Local clues, though, were scant but the Kent ARP report gave a starting point:

"15 October 1940. Time of Report: 14.25 hours. One British plane down at Albion Parade. Map Reference 090908. Pilot missing. Plane burnt out. Slight damage to wharf building."

Already, and from that information alone, it was possible to deduce that the pilot must almost certainly have been Flt Sgt Williams and by the late 1970s the RAF had confirmed it anyway. Bizarrely, the researchers now knew the final fate of Eric but, unknown to them, his widow still had no clue as to what had become of her husband or how or where he had died. To her he was still just missing.

Working with researcher Terry Thompson, the author set about tracking down Eric's family. It was a long and tortuous process involving a search for wills, birth certificates etc but, eventually, in November 1987 his widow Joan was tracked down and contacted in Ontario, Canada. Re-married, but again a widow, Joan Eddleston was staggered to learn news of what had become of her Eric. So too was Eric's daughter, Jennifer, who had never known her father – having been born shortly after his untimely death. Jennifer was, by now, a resident of the USA. It was a tragic and yet comforting situation – especially when it became clear just how important this news was to the family. At last there was now some kind of partial closure. However unsatisfactory the location of his last resting place might be, it was at least now known to them.

By 1987, and when contact with the family was established, the Protection of Military Remains Act 1986 was already in place in the UK. This meant that the expressed wishes of Eric's next of kin to have his Hurricane recovered and his body decently buried in a marked grave could *only* be met legally if a licence were granted to a recovery team by the MOD, but in cases where the presence of human remains is known or suspected it is not the policy of the MOD to grant such licenses. Notwithstanding the fact that the site owners were agreeable to a recovery taking place, it could not occur in the absence of a PMRA licence. For a while, the idea of bringing Eric Williams home had stalled.

With the possibility of recovering Eric for burial being cruelly dashed once the exact crash location had been established and next of kin traced, one of the team of researchers who had worked on the project, Dave Smith, organized the erection of a small memorial plaque to Eric in the nearby Gordon Gardens. Under the circumstances, it was the very least that could be done and it did offer some further measure of comfort for Eric's widow and daughter when they were able to visit the memorial in 1988.

By the late 1980s, however, it became clear that the long term future of the site as a timber wharf and storage area was in doubt. The busy waterfront activity on this part of the Thames was a thing of the past, and the surrounding buildings fell into disuse and dereliction. Eventually, the timber yard closed down – but not before the original wartime earthen floor had been concreted over. Realising that it was

After Eric's widow and daughter were traced and informed as to the RAF's record of his crash site, this small memorial plaque was erected by Dave Smith of the Medway Aviation Research Group in nearby Gordon Gardens. Here it is viewed by Eric's widow Joan Eddlestone and daughter Jennifer Fergus.

potentially now-or-never, the team of enthusiasts who had worked towards the recovery of Eric made another attempt, officially, to get something done. Again their efforts were thwarted. Instead, by 1995 and with the future of the site becoming increasingly doubtful, one of the research team, Mark Kirby, took matters further and obtained the following written submission from Eric's widow:

"To Whom It May Concern:
    I give my approval for Mark Kirby to locate and recover the body of Flight Sergeant Eric Edward Williams, Service No 562960, killed in action on 15th October 1940 and whose plane is believed to have crashed at Barton's Timber Wharf, Gravesend, Kent. Signed: Joan Eddleston 19 June 1995."

Walter Holden, the elderly witness, again accompanied Mark to the site and pointed out, absolutely emphatically, where the fighter had disappeared into the ground – just inside the yard gate and just off the Albion Parade roadway. Then, in the 1990s, the building was still standing and little had changed apart from the recent addition of a concrete floor and the extension of the Thames riverbank when a post-war sea wall was constructed, thereby increasing the distance from the actual crash site to the river. However, the situation was academic. Notwithstanding Joan's wishes, and the compliance of the site owner, nothing could proceed without a licence. And no licence was forthcoming.

Frustrated, the team ultimately wrote to the Ministry of Defence in 1997 seeking an official attempt at recovery. The result was not encouraging; the MOD declined to act and stated their reasons in writing to a team member. It is difficult not to view the cold harsh approach of officialdom with some dismay. Here was a case where a young pilot had given literally his all for his country and left behind a grieving wife and baby daughter. Now it seemed that the main consideration for the government was financial. Fortunately, Eric Williams and his like did not consider the likely cost when they went into battle during 1940. The Ministry of Defence wrote the following:

> "We have always felt that if we make an exception for one then the floodgates would be opened; the resources and cost involved in such an operation would be too horrendous to contemplate. We just do not have those resources."

Again, the project had hit a brick wall. Then, something happened that sparked yet more pressure on the authorities finally to do something about the Williams case. On Sunday 8 February 1998, two enthusiasts gained access to the now derelict site and carried out an unauthorized and unlicensed dig with a mechanical excavator. They found nothing. Again, the MOD were prodded into action by this surprise turn of events and were asked to review their position *vis-à-vis* an official MOD dig. Ultimately, the site was surveyed by the Royal Engineers and RAF who reported to the RAF Personnel Management Agency at RAF Innsworth on their findings. By March 1999 the MOD had responded, stating that no recovery would be attempted on the basis of the difficulties associated with the site and the potential costs. Blue One would remain missing.

For almost ten years the matter rested there. In that time Eric's widow had sadly passed away, her wish to have her husband recovered and buried not having been brought to fruition in her lifetime. Meanwhile, the site and surrounding area descended into further decay and dereliction and the buildings of the former Barton's Timber Wharf were demolished leaving just the concrete floor. Not really a fitting resting place for one of The Few.

However, in October 2006 it was revealed that the site, finally, was due for extensive re-development with luxury riverside apartments scheduled for the Albion Parade site with architects Kiran Curtis Associates drawing up detailed proposals. Local aviation historian and aircraft restorer, Lewis Deal MBE, became aware of the plans and, knowing the existence of the buried Hurricane and its pilot, mounted a campaign to have something done before Eric's remains became unreachable. At once, the team who had worked so hard on the case since the early 1980s came together and offered whatever help they could to Lewis in his laudable quest. Ultimately, Lewis pressed for the MOD and developers to concede that, now, something *must* be done. Accordingly, plans were put in hand to take matters forward.

Somewhat surprisingly, though, it was not to be an official recovery attempt *per-se*. Instead, a licence was granted to Lewis Deal as a private individual to carry out the recovery. However, the RAF and army would assist with resources and a military presence. As the plans gathered momentum, the author and Mark Kirby re-established contact with Eric's relatives, conducted a UK-based cousin to the crash site at the MOD's request and prepared a large dossier of material for Eric's daughter, Jennifer, in the USA.

Unable to trace or contact the relatives themselves, the MOD called on the services of the author to put the parties in touch – a request that was gladly complied with. At last, it seemed, things were moving forward. With the precise information that the original team had gathered, there was a high degree of confidence that the site could be located exactly – or, at least, sufficiently close to allow it to be found using the collective expertise of highly experienced aviation archaeologists, high-tech equipment and a team who were all highly motivated and dedicated to the task in hand. Unfortunately, that was not to be.

In a move that surprised the original team, and indeed the family, it was announced during July 2007 that a recovery attempt would be made in the next few days. Indeed, Wing Commander Lainchbury, Commandant of the MOD Fire Services Central Training Establishment at Manston, appeared on Meridian TV to state that the wreckage had definitely been detected at just a few metres and that work would be carried out over the weekend of 28/29 July 2007. However, when the author called the family to discuss this news they were taken aback as they knew nothing of any such plan. After a telephone call to the MOD they were assured that work was *not* going ahead as the RAF/RE team had *not* yet located the buried wreckage! Since this was contrary to what had been stated on Meridian TV, and in light of yet *another* TV report which showed preparation work at the site, the family again contacted the MOD who, this time, conceded that work was indeed going ahead after all. The reason behind the apparent obfuscation remains a mystery. At short notice the UK-based family members drove to the excavation site to witness proceedings over the duration of that weekend.

Members of the original team who had worked on the case also travelled to the site but, on arrival, were immediately denied access by RAF Police guarding the gate and a large screen was thrown up around the yard. However, it soon became very apparent to those of that team outside the periphery – and who could gain a very limited view from certain vantage points – that the dig was not in the correct place by a long way. It seemed likely that the recovery team had been misled by the location of the existing sea wall (although they were aware of the 30-metre extension to the bank) and the subsequent demolition of the building. The reference point of the bank was no longer in the position it took during 1940. This fact was clearly evident from aerial photographs of the site in the 1940s as compared to those currently available on Google Earth.

Unfortunately, the digging team appeared disinterested in engaging in dialogue with those who had extensive and long standing knowledge of the site and, indeed, of such challenging recovery operations as this. Ultimately, by the end of day two on Sunday 29 July nothing had been found. The detected readings were discovered to be the remains of an

In the summer of 2007 a Royal Air Force team from Manston and a Royal Engineer party from Chatham engaged in ultimately unsuccessful attempts to recover the Hurricane and Eric's body before the site was re-developed. The attempt failed – possibly because the team were partly misled by the present line of the sea wall, by the subsequent demolition of reference points and by failing to interpret what the period reports tell us.

Unfortunately, the official team in 2007 were singularly disinclined to enter into any dialogue with researchers who had looked into the case across a period of more than thirty years and held invaluable information and documentary evidence. Although sophisticated search equipment from Defence Science & Technology Laboratory, Fort Halstead, was used on site, the author believes that the search and excavation areas were in wholly the wrong place.

old Thames barge. It had already been long established by the original team that Thames barges were pulled up alongside the old sea wall, sunk, and then in-filled and covered over. These formed the basis of the post-war sea wall construction. The very discovery of the barge, therefore, would alone seem to have indicated an incorrect position for the excavation. However, before the site was closed down, a small service of commemoration was held which involved a moving flypast by a Battle of Britain Memorial Flight Hurricane. It was not, though, the end of matters.

Writing to the author on 30 July 2007, Wing Commander Lainchbury stated that:

"The only potential solution would involve an unacceptable scale of impact upon both the local businesses and infrastructure and would require a significant amount of ultra-expensive plant. Even then the chances of success would be no better than 50/50. Accordingly, I have recommended that no further licenses to excavate this site are issued to anyone and that the file should therefore be closed. This view is supported by the current landowner and the future developers."

This aerial photograph of the Albion Parade site at Gravesend was taken some time shortly after the crash. It shows damage to the roof (ringed) caused by the crashing fighter. The straight line represents the present sea wall, some yards from its irregular 1940 course.

Later, and on the MOD's own news website, an emphatic Wing Commander Lainchbury is quoted as saying: "I can rule out us ever going back."

To all intents and purposes, therefore, a line was officially being drawn under the case. To the family, the view was expressed that the buried wreckage was "too deep" to recover and had been "sucked under the Thames" by years of tidal action. These are not views that in the author's opinion have any credibility – either from a historical or scientific perspective. Unfortunately, there was another regrettable twist in store when, on 30 July 2007, *The Guardian* newspaper rather incredibly carried a news article headlined: "Battle of Britain Pilot's Remains Recovered at Fourth Attempt". Although they had apparently acted upon MOD press office information, the newspaper published an apology to the family on 1 August following this author's intervention. The story, released by the MOD, was wholly incorrect and it was impossible to comprehend how on earth the ministry press office could have made such a howling error. Once again the case of a missing Battle of Britain pilot was courting publicity for all the wrong reasons.

Not satisfied with the dig outcome, especially in light of their unshakeable certainty that the impact point had been entirely missed, the original team – in conjunction with the next of kin – felt strongly that the search should not now be abandoned. This view was cemented as team members escorted Eric's grand-daughter Robyn Fergus to the site during early August when she visited from the USA. It was decided there and then that Mark Kirby would apply for a licence to recover the aircraft on behalf of the family and exactly as Eric's widow Joan had originally wished. At the same time the author was formally appointed by the next of kin to represent the family's interests with the MOD.

Given that the licence holder, Lewis Deal, had written to the author to say that he no longer had an interest in pursuing the matter, it was clear that further work could not be conducted by the team working with Lewis Deal under his existing license. Thus, Mark Kirby's application was formally submitted on 25 August but on Battle of Britain Day, 2007, came the depressing news that Mark's application was being refused on the grounds that "….a licence was already in place to another party and it was not the MOD's policy to issue duplicate licenses in respect of specific sites." Not unreasonably the team took this statement from the MOD to mean that the licence referred to was that already in place for Mr Deal, but then the MOD wrote by e-mail on 21 September to say that the author's "assumption about the identity of the licence holder was incorrect".

This puzzling piece of information persuaded the team again to consult Mr Deal, but before that could be done there was yet another twist in the increasingly bizarre quest to recover Eric Williams when, the very next day, on Saturday 22 September, the same MOD officer telephoned the family to say another attempt was being made to recover the Hurricane that very day – starting immediately! This flew in the face of Wing Commander Lainchbury's emphatic statement about the formal abandonment of the site a few months earlier. Stunned by this sudden and unexpected piece of news the family members drove at once to the site.

Again, digging over a two-day period yielded absolutely nothing but mud, rubble and scrap iron – and not a trace of the Hurricane or of Eric. Again, one of the original team members who had been instrumental in the adjacent memorial, and who had a veritable wealth of knowledge and experience, attempted vainly to impart the vitally important information he had. He was not even allowed into the site.

Interpretation of maps, aerial photographs, the measuring of fixed locations on the ground and the use of GPS makes an approximation of the site position relatively easy, especially when used in conjunction with crucial and invaluable eye witness information from one who worked at the wharf but who is now long since dead. Indeed, the points excavated thus far seemed to be off track by a significant margin when compared against building and site boundaries, fixed reference points and the testimony of William Holden who had been pretty emphatic about the crash position – not to mention the description of the location as reported to the RAF's No 49 Maintenance Unit.

This surprise new excavation was conducted by none other than Wing Commander David Lainchbury who, according to newspaper reports, was acting on information that had come to light from a new witness. Against the background of Lainchbury's earlier and very definite statements about the future of the site, and his ruling out ever going back, this news of a re-dig was rather astonishing to say the least. Certainly, the spot excavated was much nearer to the actual crash site – but *again* it was missed. As it turned out, Wing Commander Lainchbury was now the licence holder, the licence remaining in force for one year. Again, the new dig was only a quasi-military affair.

Apart from the use of government-owned hi-tec location equipment, this last dig also relied on 'new' information supplied by one of those who had taken part in the unauthorised excavation attempt of February 1988. Since that effort had singularly failed to recover any wreckage or to identify the exact spot and had also been conducted following unauthorised access to the site – both apparently without landowner's consent or a

REPORT TO SQUADRON LEADER GOODMAN
R.A.F. DEPOT 17-10-40.

HURRICANE V 6550.   Bartons Timber Yard, Albion Parade E. of Gravesend.

I located the site where the above aircraft crashed and spoke to the yard
foreman and local Police officer. They informed me that the Hurricane had crashed
through the roof of the timber store and buried itself deeply in the dirt floor. Upon
inspection I found a crater in the floor caused by the crashing aircraft. Small parts were
scattered around and I collected these together to leave for later collection. A large
section of wing had been retrieved from the roof. I deposited a quantity of bullets into
the river. A party of Royal Engineers had been digging some several feet into the crater
to find the pilot but had given up due to water ingress and collapse. Before leaving I
supervised the probing of the crater using a long metal pole and boat – hook. I could
touch wreckage about ten feet down. Although the site is only about fifteen or twenty
feet inside the yard gate and access is easy it will be difficult if not impossible to recover
the engine.

I have instructed a gang to clear remaining debris today 18th October and take to I.T.C.
Sandling Park. I await your further instructions.

Signed   _____

Another valuable report from the archives of A V Nicholls & Co is this one relating to the
crash at Albion Parade. It is quite specific in relation to positioning the crash location. If that
report was accurate and the recall of the late Walter Holden was spot on, then it gives
considerable clarity to the position of the buried wreckage – some distance from the areas
excavated in 2007.

Having apparently smashed through the timber roof at an angle, the Hurricane then
impacted into the floor in the extreme south-west corner of the existing yard although it
may, just, be under an adjacent and more recently constructed warehouse. Only time will tell
which report is accurate – if and when the site comes under further official investigation
ahead of planned large-scale re-development of the locality for new housing.

Protection of Military Remains Act Licence – it can only be described as utterly bewildering
that the MOD should then have relied upon one of those involved in that 1988 attempt to
provide them with reliable information! The more so in that information held by others,
including one who had been appointed by the family as their representative, could have
been available to the authorities and would most likely have pointed in a more accurate
direction.

In 1940, the Royal Engineer party had given up digging when it became too dangerous
at eighteen feet. Later, a party from 49 Maintenance Unit (RAF) visited to clear away what
little remained there. Loose rounds of .303 ammunition were thrown into the river and
pieces of wing structure taken away and dumped at Sandling Park, the scraps not being
worth conveying back to the RAF Faygate depot. Before they left, the squad probed into

the crater with a boat hook and metal pipe and described the spot as "…just inside the yard entrance" going on to tell how they struck a solid mass of wreckage at ten feet. That is where it lays to this day.

At time of writing, the case remains in a state of apparent impasse although a small remembrance event organized by the original team was held at Eric's nearby memorial on 11 November 2007, attended by his daughter, Jennifer, the local MP, Adam Holloway, and others involved in the project over a span of many years. Holloway, in fact, was emphatic that no building should be started on the site until Eric Williams had been found, and if he could not be then the site should not be developed. It was an emotive event where it was hard not to reflect on Wing Commander David Lainchbury's earlier statement that any future attempt will stand less than a 50/50 chance of success. The odds faced by The Few were considerably shorter than that, but Eric Williams and his like did not give up. One must hope that those involved with any future attempt to locate the Hurricane at Barton's Wharf in order to bring Eric home will continue to show a similar spirit of determination.

CHAPTER 13 Found But Still Missing…

E ACH YEAR, on the Sunday nearest to 3 September, an elaborate and moving ceremony is held on the edge of an orchard at Chart Sutton, Kent, to honour a Battle of Britain pilot killed there on 3 September 1940. Local dignitaries, the RAF Association, Air Training Corps and villagers gather around a memorial garden. Beautifully planted and maintained in this remote corner of Kent, a wooden cross stands at the centre of the flower beds. The cross is simply engraved "RAF Pilot – September 3rd 1940". A short service is held, wreaths are laid and a Hurricane aircraft of the Battle of Britain Memorial Flight dips low overhead in salute to the "Unknown Airman".

The story of the event dates back to 1940 when, on 3 September, a Hurricane plunged out of one of the many air battles above and buried itself deep in the heavy clay. Its unknown pilot had not escaped and a couple who lived nearby placed a simple wooden cross at the site and laid flowers there at each anniversary. With the passage of time the memorial fell into disrepair and

Pilot Officer Robert Henry Shaw of 1 Squadron RAF, who died when his Hurricane crashed at Chart Sutton on 3 September 1940 and whose crash location is now marked by a memorial garden.

the now elderly couple eventually passed away but in 1970 the nearby Headcorn branch of the RAFA resurrected the memorial, restored the garden and kept it permanently maintained and began the now traditional service. Aside from a brief entry in the Maidstone Civil Defence Book in the Kent County archives little was known about the crash. That entry read: "British Fighter down in flames near Park House, Chart Sutton, 10.42 hours. Map ref

The Unknown Airman's Grave memorial garden at Chart Sutton, Kent. Note the recording of the date on the cross – 3 September 1940.

21/73." A further message timed at 11.12 hours recorded: "Aircraft still burning fiercely. Machine gun bullets exploding. Still no news of pilot."

When the memorial was resurrected in 1970, that was about all that was known of the crash – save for the fact that local legend had it that this had been a Hurricane. Each year, on the same Sunday, the memorial service was held to honour this unidentified pilot. The site became known as the "Airman's Grave". In a sense it was just that. In a sense, too, it almost became the Battle of Britain equivalent to the Tomb of The Unknown Soldier, although here the high vaulted sky that had claimed this pilot's life had become the cathedral roof that covered it. In its simplicity and its stunningly beautiful location, with wide panoramic views out across the Kent countryside, the memorial seemed more than fittingly appropriate in its representation of all the pilots who had died in these skies during the Battle of Britain. There was really no intention to name this man. In 1970 – and earlier – that seemed impossible anyway. In any event, the whole point of the memorial garden was its representation of a missing man. Nonetheless, there was always a degree of curiosity as to who he might be.

The work of Brighton-based haulage contractors A V Nicholls & Co has been mentioned previously and was an operation whereby the company was contracted to the Air Ministry to help clear away aircraft wrecks – British and German – from their scattered crash sites in south-east England. The company had been engaged in 1940, when the number of wrecks that had to be cleared simply overwhelmed the RAF's own resources. In 1972, however, the author contacted the former proprietor of that company, Arthur Nicholls, and discovered that he still held all of his wartime notes and records. Nicholls was only too happy to hand them over, pleased that his carefully preserved notes might be of some interest. Of interest they certainly were! Contained within the file were orders for the collection of specific wrecks and detailed reports on what had been found or recovered and compiled by Arthur Nicholls himself. It was a treasure-trove of data that enabled detail to be added to many losses of the Battle of Britain, including serial numbers and precise crash locations. Amongst the losses detailed was a Hurricane at Chart Sutton.

In a report dated 29 September 1940 to Squadron Leader Goodman, Nicholls filed the following:

REPORT TO SQUADRON LEADER GOODMAN
R.A.F. DEPOT. 29-9-40.

HURRICANE P 3782.   Parkhouse Farm, Chart, Sutton.

I located site of crash as above, inspected crater made by aircraft with P.C. Whyman No: 165, Kent County Constabulary, stationed at Sutton Vallence. He informed me that this aircraft was removed by an R.A.F. Squad with a long, low, loader on Saturday the 28th September. This P.C. found billeting accommodation for the Squad. The site has been completely cleared.

Signed _____A V Nicholls_____

The report of Arthur Nicholls to the RAF's 49 Maintenance Unit at Faygate, Sussex, which records the aircraft serial number and thereby establishes the identity of the pilot.

Park House Farm is, indeed, the location of the airman's memorial and the additional information as to the serial number of the Hurricane, P3782, suddenly revealed the identity of the unknown airman. P3782 was a Hurricane of 1 Squadron RAF and had been lost on the morning of 3 September 1940 during a squadron patrol. Its pilot, Pilot Officer Robert Henry Shaw, was posted missing and was never found. Consequently, Shaw's name can be found on the Runnymede Memorial although, in reality, evidence exists as to where he still lies. This discovery, of course, rather put into question the continuance of the ceremony to honour an unknown airman. How to deal with the situation posed a dilemma for the author. Should he simply bury the detail that had emerged and forget about it? Or should he take the matter forward in some way? Having considered many of the other cases that had gone before, and the undying gratitude of relatives who had been able to discover what had happened to loved ones, the choice was not a difficult one. The family of Robert Shaw had to be told. First though, they had to be found.

According to his birth certificate, Robert Henry Shaw was born on 28 July 1916 to Colin and Ida Shaw at Astley Bridge, Bolton. Other than that, any clue as to the family whereabouts was non-existent. To add to the difficulties the surname Shaw was hardly uncommon. Looking for the Shaw family was like the proverbial needle in a haystack, but an appeal by the author in the *Bolton Evening News* during May 1987 quickly drew results. Before very long, contact had been established with Robert's two surviving brothers; Lt Col William Shaw and Thomas Shaw, and his sisters Catherine Cornish and Alison Barton. All were immediately apprised of the situation regarding their long-missing brother and were sent copies of all the supporting documentary evidence.

All the siblings were convinced by the evidence presented to them, but remained puzzled as to how or why their brother should still be missing. Clear evidence existed to support the view that here was their brother's aeroplane. On top of that, it was well known locally that the pilot was still in the wreckage. Even the date of the crash was known with that all important detail carved onto the memorial cross. Under the circumstances it is hard to explain why Robert was left in situ, but the clue probably lies within the report submitted by Arthur Nicholls after he had visited the site on 29 September 1940. It reads:

"Hurricane P3782. Parkhouse Farm. Chart Sutton.
I located site of crash as above, inspected crater made by aircraft with P.C. Whyman, no.165, Kent County Constabulary, stationed in Sutton Vallence. He informed me that this aircraft was removed by an RAF squad with a long low-loader on Saturday the 28th September. This P.C. found billeting for the squad. The site has been completely cleared.
Signed: A V Nicholls"

Mr Nicholls took no further action, understandably believing that the site had been fully cleared and there was nothing else for him to take away. What he did not realise, of course, was that the RAF squad who had beaten him to it by one day had merely cleared away the surface wreckage leaving the engine and fuselage deeply embedded in the ground. Ex-police constable Mr R F Whyman was still living in November 1978 and was traced to Brighton by the author. His recall of the event was clear and he could confirm what had happened: "I do know that a plane was brought down at Park House Farm, Chart Sutton, on 3 September 1940. The engine was buried in the Wealden clay and I think it was never recovered."

Without a doubt, then, the engine must have still been buried when Arthur Nicholls left the site on 29 September. With it was buried the fuselage, cockpit and the unfortunate Robert Shaw. Nicholls' report to Squadron Leader Goodman simply drew an official line under the case and Pilot Officer Shaw was destined to remain classified as missing in action – his parents duly notified that no trace of him could be found. Wing Commander 'Pat' Hancock, then secretary to the Battle of Britain Fighter Association, was flying with Robert

Shaw on the day in question. Writing in October 1978 he recalled:

> "I have referred to my log book and on 3 September 1940 I was flying with Flt Lt Hillcoat, B Flight Commander, and Pilot Officer Shaw. I recorded the sortie north of Dungeness and that both pilots were missing. So you are right, and poor old Shaw is still with his aeroplane."

The Shaw family, however, were now faced with making a collective decision as to what should be done. Ultimately, it fell to Lt Col Shaw to announce that they had decided to maintain the status quo. He wrote:

> "The RAF Association at Headcorn have over a number of years maintained this memorial and built up the wreath-laying ceremony which has now become a local institution. This ceremony, it seems to us, owes its local popularity in great part to the mystique of an unknown pilot. This would not be the same if the pilot were officially known. We also have in mind what we think would have been our brother's feelings on the matter but are content to now know where he lies. Had it not been for your investigations and hard work in taking the trouble to find us then we would never have known. And knowing is very important to us."

It was an entirely understandable decision and Lt Col Shaw's response on behalf of the family clearly hid some considerable emotion between the lines he had written. Having met this very correct retired officer it was clear that emotion was not something he found easy to countenance or deal with, although it is interesting to note that after making this decision members of the Shaw family, including Lt Col Shaw, have travelled each year to the memorial service. As the years have passed so that tradition has continued down into subsequent generations. Generations who were not even born when Robert Shaw had died.

Strangely, there is also a tacit acknowledgement that this is the grave of Robert Shaw by the organisers and participants of the annual service and, of course, by family members who are welcomed on most years at the ceremony by the RAF Association. As the other brother Thomas Shaw put it: "Our brother Bobbie is here. We are sure of that, but he represents all of the other pilots who didn't come back in 1940. It isn't just his memorial. It belongs to them all."

Eight days after Robert Shaw failed to return another Hurricane pilot was shot down over Kent and posted missing. This time it was a pilot from 504 Squadron, Pilot Officer Arthur William Clarke, who had failed to return. As was the case with each casualty, the first terse notification that a pilot was missing came in a brief and formal telegram to the next of kin. Invariably that was followed up by a letter of condolence from the commanding officer and at times during 1940 various COs were kept busy writing letters to grieving parents or wives. It must have been an awful and draining task. In the case of Arthur Clarke the letter was written by Squadron Leader John Sample on 19 September 1940:

"Dear Mrs Clarke

As C.O. of 504 Squadron I am just writing a short letter to let you know as best I can the circumstances in which your son is reported missing.

"As it is just over a week now since he was missing I am afraid that there is very little hope of hearing from him now. We were on patrol over Kent when we intercepted about thirty enemy bombers with escort fighters and attacked about ten miles west of Folkestone. We went into attack three at a time and your son was in the second three to attack. Nobody saw anything happen to him and after the attack we were spilt up and returned home separately as usually happens. As nobody saw anything one can really not say what happened.

"It is conceivably possible that he jumped out by parachute and was carried by the wind out into the Channel where he might have been taken prisoner by a German torpedo boat but I am afraid that is very unlikely. We all liked him very much and are very sorry he is not with us now.

"I am sorry I cannot tell you anything more than this, but nobody saw anything. I am afraid that this is very often the case in these air battles.

Yours sincerely,

J Sample

(Squadron Leader) "

As with Gruszka, Beresford, Drake and just about all the other casualties covered in this book, no fellow pilots saw the going of him. One minute he was there, in the thick of battle, the next he was gone. In John Sample's letter we have the clue that battle was joined ten miles west of Folkestone. This, as a starting point to find Arthur Clarke, is not specific enough to be particularly helpful and yet it does place his loss, or at least where he was last seen, in an *estimated* position. As it happens, ten miles west of Folkestone brings one to a point, roughly, just to the north of Newchurch in the middle of Kent's Romney Marsh. Fortunately there was a clue that something did happen on the ground, right there at Newchurch, on 11 September 1940. Mrs Ivy Homewood who lived at Wills Farm in Newchurch village and who kept a diary of events in 1940, had recorded an incident on 11 September. The short but significant entry reads: "Spitfire *(sic)* crashed in Newchurch burying itself deep in the ground."

Pilot Officer Arthur William Clarke of 504 Squadron was shot down and killed at Newchurch on Romney Marsh on 11 September 1940. His body was never found and apparently lies in the wreckage of his Hurricane buried beneath the marsh.

Despite what we can now determine to be incorrect identification as to the aircraft type, there is no doubting that the incident Ivy noted was indeed the crash of Arthur Clarke's Hurricane. Eventually other evidence would emerge to confirm so. Again it was the work of the Kent Battle of Britain Museum (whom we have also met earlier) that would provide the clinching evidence. At some time in either 1972 or 1973 the museum excavated a crash site situated at Rookelands, near Newchurch, of an aircraft wreck that turned out to be a Hurricane, unearthing a shattered Rolls-Royce Merlin engine, map box with a complete set of maps, cockpit items and equipment, a pair of pilot's silk inner gloves and a handkerchief marked CLARKE in indelible ink.

Here was the only link needed to associate the crash witnessed that day by Ivy Homewood with the loss of Pilot Officer Clarke, who was last seen "…ten miles west of Folkestone". Displayed at the Kent Battle of Britain Museum, the artefacts were clearly identified as coming from Hurricane P3770 in which Arthur Clarke was lost. Although the engine (situated in front of the pilot) was unearthed, along with other cockpit parts, no human remains were reported as being found. Once again a situation had emerged where a pilot was still missing although his fate had effectively been determined. (Gruszka and Beresford being the other two cases in point.) Some time after the excavation had been carried out a farm worker, Peter Stickells, was ploughing over the site in the 1980s and discovered a neck chain that had clearly belonged to the pilot of the Hurricane. Retrieving the item from a freshly ploughed furrow he then handed it in to the nearby Brenzett Aeronautical Museum. That the pilot had been in the Hurricane was clearly beyond any doubt. Indeed, if there *had* been any doubts about it then they were certainly not shared by Battle of Britain veteran, Squadron Leader Dave Glaser.

Writing to the chairman of the Battle of Britain Fighter Association, Air Commodore A R MacDonell, on 20 June 1975, Glaser was brutally frank:

"[another]..is Plt Off A W Clarke of 504 Squadron, shot down on 11 September 1940. Apparently his crash was dug up between October 1972 and April 1973 and once again the body put back in the hole. I have checked [with the MOD] and as far as they know he is missing, believed killed."

What had become of Arthur Clarke, or why no trace of his body was ever discovered, remains a mystery although it was not so to the landowner of the site, Brian Frith. Speaking in the 1980s he was adamant that, as far as he knew, the pilot had been found during the 1970s dig. On this point he was absolutely and totally insistent when interviewed by enthusiasts Mark Kirby and Steve Vizard. He told Kirby and Vizard that he had been there when a team had dug on his land. He recalled the engine, split open and with oil still pouring out of it, and he remembered the pilot being found too. He did not know what had happened after that. Mark Kirby recalled the conversation at Mr Frith's Warren Farm home in nearby Dymchurch:

"Mr Frith was quite angry when I suggested to him that the pilot was still missing. Basically, Mr Frith said that as he had been there when the plane wreckage was dug up he knew he had been found and that was that. It was all very odd."

Curious as to the fate of Arthur Clarke, the author set about trying to find the Clarke family since it seemed very likely that they would not know what had happened to their relative and there was clear evidence at least as to where he had lost his life. As with the case of Pilot Officer Shaw, the surname Clarke is obviously exceedingly common in the UK and there were not even any starting points to begin from. No clues existed in the Commonwealth War Graves Commission Register for the Runnymede Memorial as to where the Clarke family might have originated. The only lead was his age, recorded as just twenty. Armed with this information alone, the author trawled the indexed registers at St Catherine's House and established there were no less than thirteen Arthur W Clarkes registered as being born in the UK during 1919/1920. Which one was it? Setting aside the cost of obtaining thirteen birth certificates, the acquisition of these alone wouldn't help greatly. There would still be no clue as to which to look for and establishing that was crucially important if the quest were to be taken one stage further and an attempt made to find relatives.

Some other way had to be found and the author finally wrote to the RAF Officers Records Centre at RAF Innsworth, sending a list of all thirteen of the Arthur W Clarkes with annotated brief details of each one noted on the list. The question posed of the MOD was simple; which one is it? The reply, when it came, was at first sight slightly disappointing and stated that personal data such as this could not be disclosed to a third party. Amazingly, though, the list of thirteen Arthur W Clarkes sent to the MOD had been returned to the author with their letter and against one of those names was marked a red "X"!! This was the Arthur William Clarke born on 26 December 1919 in the Bucklow Registration District, County of Chester. The hunt was on.

As with the Shaw case, letters were published in various local newspapers and within twenty-four hours Arthur's sister, Mrs Kay Freeman, was in touch by telephone. Kay was astonished and moved by what she learnt and asked to have as much detail sent to her as possible. This was duly done and in the summer of 1986 Kay and other family members visited the crash site. Afterwards, she wrote:

> "To tell the truth I have now come to terms with the fact that Arthur lies in a farmer's field. It was a shock, but now I know. That you have spent three years trying to find us to let us know restores my faith in human nature. I only wish that mother had lived to know. She was broken hearted when he was lost. We tried to jolly her along by saying that he was only missing and that that didn't mean he was dead. We tried to say that all the time he was just missing there was hope. But she knew."

After a family conference Arthur's nearest and dearest decided that they would like a monument placed near the crash site in his memory and, in due course, a simple stone was placed by the roadside just yards from the actual location. On 11 September 1986 it was dedicated in a small ceremony, led by the parish vicar the Rev Hugh Walker, and with family and serving RAF officers present. Amongst the latter was his great nephew Flt Lt Symon Riley (a Tornado navigator) who placed a wreath for the family and saluted the memorial to his great-uncle.

Despite having being found, both Pilot Officer Shaw and Pilot Officer Clarke are still officially listed as missing.

On 11 September 1986, the Clarke family dedicated this memorial on the roadside at
Newchurch to the memory of Arthur who lies just a few yards away behind the hedge.
The design of Arthur's memorial follows very closely the lines of the CWGC standard pattern
grave headstone – although this is a private memorial and not an official CWGC one.

CHAPTER 14

Known Unto God

I N CASES where airmen were recovered for burial but not identified the Commonwealth War Graves Commission headstones are marked simply: "Known Unto God". Not in every case has the mystery of their identity endured, and it has very often been the case that research into the background as to who these unknown airmen might be has been initiated by investigations into other RAF fighter pilots downed in the vicinity of such graves – including the research into the missing casualties detailed in these pages. A case in point is that of Sgt J H M Ellis detailed in Chapter Nine.

During the early 1970s, and at a time when aviation archaeological activity was reaching its climax in south-east England, the crash site of a Spitfire came under scrutiny on Buckmans Green Farm at Smarden in Kent. The investigators this time were Tony Graves and John Tickner of the then London Air Museum. Very little was known of the history of the aeroplane except that its pilot had been shot down in flames during the Battle of Britain and its

Flight Lieutenant F W 'Rusty' Rushmer the B Flight commander of 603 Squadron, lost over Kent on 5 September 1940.

pilot killed. However, a wooden beam in an adjacent barn had been inscribed by hop-pickers or farm workers at the time of the crash with the legend: "Spitfire 5.9.1940".

John and Tony, by a simple process of deduction, had concluded that the aeroplane must have been X4261 of 603 Squadron, shot down at approximately 10.00am on 5 September 1940, resulting in the death of its pilot, Flt Lt Frederick William Rushmer. Still classified as missing, and with his name inscribed on the Runnymede Memorial, 'Rusty' Rushmer's whereabouts was officially unknown. However, an RAF war grave in the nearby All Saints Churchyard, Staplehurst, held an interesting clue. Unusually, beneath the inscription "An Airman of The Second World War" and above the text "Known Unto God" was carved a date – 5 September 1940. Further research in the church burial register revealed the following entry:

"Fragmentary remains of an unidentified airman who died as the result of enemy action on Thursday 5 September 1940. Plane crashed in Parish of Smarden, Kent. Buried 11 September 1940. Alfred J Walker. Rector."

There was only one loss in the Parish of Smarden on 5 September 1940 that could be considered. The crash at Buckmans Green Farm.

The crash site excavation by John and Tony revealed nothing by way of positive identity confirmation for either the airframe or pilot – save that it was a Spitfire and its unfortunate pilot had clearly died in the crash. An item discovered by the pair proved the latter point and was to prove crucial in later identification efforts. That item was a silver half-hunter pocket watch. In 1980, Battle of Britain historian and writer, Peter Cornwell, first linked the crash site excavated by the London Air Museum to the Staplehurst grave and to Flt Lt Rushmer, but it was not until the artefacts recovered by John and Tony were acquired by the Tangmere Aviation Museum in 1980 (when the London Air Museum folded) that matters took a step forward.

Keenly interested in the various mysteries of missing aircrew from the Battle of Britain period the author, then curator at Tangmere Museum, set about trying to prove the link and thereby the identity of the pilot. It was

The half-hunter pocket watch recovered from the crash site in the 1970s. It had stopped at exactly the time Rushmer was known to have been shot down and was recognised by his sisters as identical to the one he had owned.

a quest that lasted almost eighteen years and, initially, involved tracking down Rushmer's next-of-kin. As with many casualties of the period, the CWGC registers held no clue as to next of kin, home town or age. However, the author's extensive search of indexes at St Catherine's House in 1986 for the period 1900 to 1920 (during which period it was assumed that Rushmer must have been born) revealed a Frederick William Rushmer born on 12 May 1910. It was the only F W Rushmer and it had to be the same person. The birth was registered as having been at Lodge Farm, Sisland. A simple check of telephone directories in that area revealed a Muriel Rushmer living near Beccles in Suffolk. She turned out to be Flt Lt Rushmer's sister. Writing to the author in August 1987, Miss Rushmer told how she had discussed the research material the author had put to her with her two sisters, Agnes and Margaret. All three had agreed that the Staplehurst grave must be their brother's last resting place and petitioned the MOD and CWGC, with the author, to have the Staplehurst grave duly accepted and marked as Flt Lt Rushmer's.

The rationale for concluding that this must be his grave was simple. There were only two missing casualties lost in Spitfires that day: Sqn Ldr 'Robin' Hood of 41 Squadron and Flt Lt 'Rusty' Rushmer. However, both had vanished at distinctly different geographical locations and at different times.

Rushmer and his 603 Squadron were involved in a huge melee with Me 109s at approximately 1000hrs in the Maidstone area, a battle from which the respected and much-loved B Flight commander had failed to return. Officially, no trace of him was ever found. Later that day, at approximately 1500hrs, Sqn Ldr Hood led his 41 Squadron Spitfires into battle over Essex and somewhere near Billericay. Writing in 1987, Sqn Ldr Ben Bennions (then a pilot officer with 41 Squadron) recalled events:

"On 5 September 1940 'Robin' Hood was leading the squadron – both in the morning *and* the afternoon. During the afternoon both Hood and Terry Webster, our B Flight commander, were killed. Norman Ryder, the A Flight commander, thought they may have collided whilst trying to avoid an attack by Me 109s. I'm afraid I did not see what happened. We were in a line astern. I was about tenth in line and we carried out a head-on attack on a formation of Me 109s and He 111s. It was utterly chaotic!! I think we were just north of the Thames Estuary at the time and it would have been approximately 3.00 to 3.30pm."

Bennions' testimony is important as it provides evidence that Hood was still alive until at least 3pm that day and it is known from local ARP records that the Buckmans Green casualty was killed around 1000hrs – the approximate time at which Rushmer disappeared. Adding further evidence to this was the half-hunter pocket watch which had stopped at about ten minutes past ten. In addition, Fred Rushmer's sisters all had a clear recollection that their brother had owned a watch identical to the one found by Tony Graves and John Tickner and that this had been a 21st Birthday gift from their late father. The official MOD stance in 1987, though, remained implacable; there had been two RAF casualties that day in Spitfires. Both were missing. The Staplehurst grave could be either of the two.

Compounding the difficulties experienced in getting the matter finally resolved, the RAF's Air Historical Branch had stated that the casualty reports for Hood gave the time of his loss as 0940hrs and for Rushmer as 1000hrs. Clearly, the time recorded for Hood was in error and apart from Bennions' testimony the reports contained within 41 Squadron's operations record book helped confirm matters. Nevertheless, attempts to resolve the case continued to fall on stony ground until, in August 1997, the CWGC information officer, Barry Murphy, contacted the author to say that the MOD and CWGC were "close" to accepting the evidence presented to them on the matter but were still seeking further evidence that might yet conclusively prove that the grave was Rushmer's and not Hood's. Collating all the reports and correspondence that had been assembled, including the evidence of the watch and the joint testimonies of the Misses Rushmer, the author submitted a final dossier for the CWGC's consideration.

Within a matter of weeks the CWGC had announced that they were now happy to accept the evidence and that, at last, a named headstone would be erected to replace that of the unknown airman at Staplehurst. The first public release of this information came in journalist John Crossland's article in *The Sunday Telegraph* on Battle of Britain Sunday, 14 September 1997. Oddly, the story was picked up by the Battle of Britain Historical Society who, for their own reasons, fiercely denounced John Crossland's piece as wholly untrue in their own in-house publication, *The Boblet*, during September 1997. At best, said the Battle of Britain Historical Society, *The Sunday Telegraph* story was a case of "unfortunate journalistic licence of the very worst kind". By May 1998, however, a new CWGC headstone had been erected over the grave at All Saints Churchyard, Staplehurst, bearing the name of Flt Lt F W Rushmer.

The new headstone erected at Staplehurst Churchyard in Kent during May 1998 to Flt Lt F W Rushmer, replacing the previous stone to an unknown RAF airman. The replacement of this stone was based upon research carried out by the author and submitted to the relevant authorities.

The records that had been supplied to the author by the late Arthur Nicholls detailing his work as a civilian haulage contractor for the Air Ministry salvaging the wrecks of downed aircraft, have already been shown as invaluable in unravelling various mysteries relating to missing Battle of Britain pilots. Whilst they did not help in the case of Flt Lt Rushmer, they were key to clearing up yet another matter where a Battle of Britain pilot had been buried as an unknown airman. This was the case of Fg Off J W Cutts, a Spitfire pilot of 222 Squadron posted missing on 4 September 1940.

An appendix to a letter from Sqn Ldr Goodman to Arthur Nicholls reproduced on page 146, which held the key to the Shaw mystery (see Chapter Thirteen) also unlocked the case of John Cutts. The entry directly above that referring to Robert Shaw's Hurricane (P3782) reads: "Spitfire K4278. Amberfield Farm. Chart Sutton." *(In fact, the entry should have* *read **X4278** as K4278 was a Tiger Moth of 24 Squadron lost in a crash at Melton Mowbray on 15 March 1937 and so can be discounted completely.)*

Since X4278 is known to be the Spitfire in which Fg Off J W Cutts was lost, it yet again throws up the now familiar question; if this is where his aircraft crashed then what happened to the still missing pilot? His loss had been reported by the Bognor newspapers in September 1940, where the following was announced:

"Bognor Pilot Officer Missing.
Mr J W Cutts
    We regret to record that John Wintringham Cutts, aged 20, a Pilot Officer of the Royal Air Force, and the younger son of Mr & Mrs J W Cutts has been reported officially as missing. Mr J W Cutts (senior) is the well known Bognor solicitor.
    Bognorians will join us in extending sympathy to Mr & Mrs Cutts with the hope that good news of their son may be received in the near future."

Sadly, no such good news was ever forthcoming and unlike some of the other cases we can now discount the possibility that his remains were, or are, still with the aircraft. Indeed, the crash site itself was subject to excavation by the Brenzett Aeronautical Museum during 1972 when the badly burnt wreckage was uncovered – the most significant being a propeller hub and blade. Very little of the aircraft actually remained there. Of the pilot there was no trace and yet it was known that he was missing. The answer to the mystery was to be found not many miles away at Bell Road (Milton) Cemetery, Sittingbourne.

Here, in Plot W.143, could be found the remains of an unknown RAF airman with the burial register showing this casualty to have come from Amberfield Farm and having been buried at Sittingbourne by the Rev A Jones on 28 September 1940. The death certificate for this casualty further shows that the body of the unknown RAF

Pilot Officer J W Cutts of 222 Squadron, lost over Kent in his Spitfire on 4 September 1940.

pilot was found on 14 September at Amberley (sic) Farm. More than fifty years later the author was able to put together all of the pieces of this particular puzzle and match them to the report about Spitfire X4278 at Amberfield Farm. Very clearly the RAF had identified by serial number this particular crashed Spitfire but in the fog of war had inexplicably failed to make any connection with John Cutts.

Spitfires of 222 and 603 Squadrons at RAF Hornchurch, late August 1940. Nearest is ZD-D, X4278. This was the aircraft in which Pilot Officer J W Cutts was lost. The next Spitfire, XT-M, is the Spitfire in which Pilot Officer Richard Hillary was shot down on 3 September. It is known that Hillary had been having difficulty in sliding back his canopy and work had been on-going to rectify this. In this view XT-M is clearly being worked on and there are open toolboxes and fitters in attendance. Interestingly, the canopy is only partly open [or has been removed?] and is not slid fully back to the radio mast. In the author's opinion we are looking here at a photograph depicting the very scenario Hillary describes in *The Last Enemy*)

The sad result was that the Cutts' family endured the pain of uncertain loss. Maybe they eventually accepted that he must have died, but they could have no knowledge as to where or how he had died. Neither could they have imagined that he was, indeed, already buried in an English cemetery deep in the heart of Kent not too many miles from his Sussex home. And all of this due to administrative failures in making any link between the casualty and his aeroplane. By 1999, however, the muddle that had been exposed by the author had filtered through to the MOD and CWGC with the result that a new headstone was placed over Plot W.143 bearing the name of Fg Off J W Cutts. It was too late for John Cutts's nearest and dearest, though, because although the author had been in touch with immediate family members in the 1980s all of them had died by 1999. However, two more of The Few were no longer missing although – as ever – there was a postscript to one of the cases.

Many years after the Brenzett Aeronautical Museum's excavation at the crash site of what is now known to have been John Cutts's Spitfire, Mark Kirby visited Amberfield Farm to view the scene of the incident. Curiosity drew him there. He didn't go to dig, but looking down something caught his eye laying on the soil. It appeared to be a badly bent penny. He picked it up and took it home but after cleaning off the mud and verdigris, he discovered it to be a neck pendant or charm of some kind and not a penny after all. There was little

No.49 Maintenance Unit,
Royal Air Force,
Faygate, Horsham, SUSSEX.

Ref:-49MU/1805/Eng.   19th September, 1940.

A.V.Nicholls Esq., M.I.B.E.
District Transport Office,
Princes House,
North Street,
BRIGHTON.1.

Dear Sirs,

        Confirming telephone instructions, herewith
authority to collect the following aircraft and deliver
to this Unit;for further delivery instructions:-

Hurricane. Spit End, Elmley, Isle of Sheppey.
Fighter.   Harty Sidings, Sheppey.
Hurricane. Hollingbourne.
Spitfire.X.4034. Wyldage Farm,Bludbean, Kent.
Spitfire.K.4278. Amberfield Farm, Chart Sutton.
Hurricane.P.3782. Park House Farm, Chart Sutton.

                    Yours faithfully,

                    L.O.Goodman
                    Squadron Leader, Commanding,
                    No.49 Maintenance Unit, R.A.F.

The report from the archives of A V Nicholls & Co that confirms the serial number and crash location of John Cutts's Spitfire. This enabled a link to be established with the grave of an unknown RAF airman at Sittingbourne and convinced the Ministry of Defence and Commonwealth War Graves Commission to change the headstone to one bearing his name. Thus, another Battle of Britain pilot is no longer missing. The value of these reports has been immense in clearing up a number of outstanding mysteries relating to missing Battle of Britain aircrew and without them many cases would remain unsolved.

doubt that it had originated from the crash – impact damage to the medallion told him that. After cleaning it carefully, a decoration of angels was clearly visible on one side. On the other side a verse from Psalms emerged from the dirt. By coincidence this is the very same text from the scriptures that is shown on a scroll being held by two angels depicted in the stained glass window at the Runnymede memorial (see page 183). Just a few feet away, on Panel 5 of the monument, is engraved the name of Pilot Officer J W Cutts.

Whilst these two cases were solved there is at least one other that has defied every attempt to unravel its mysteries. This involves an unknown airman who, originally buried on the foreshore at Camber, was re-buried at Northiam Cemetery in East Sussex on 22 September 1940. Here, a lonely CWGC headstone is inscribed:

An Airman of the 1939-45 War
Buried on 22 September 1940
Known Unto God

So who was this casualty from Camber-on-Sea? And where did he come from? First, we need to consider a geographical anomaly that may have some bearing in advancing further any possible theories. To the *west* of Rye Harbour and on the flat marshland immediately to the north of Winchelsea Beach is to be found Camber Castle – but it is *not* actually *in* Camber. Camber itself is situated well to the *east* of Rye Harbour and on the other side of the River Rother egress into Rye Bay. So, we have two possible locations that the CWGC might be trying to explain in their register – Camber Castle (which is situated on a beach) or Camber itself. Each location throws up a possible casualty but, technically, there is no such place as "Camber-on-Sea"!

At Camber Castle we do have the crash of an 85 Squadron Hurricane on 29 August 1940 which took the life of Flt Lt H R 'Hammy' Hamilton. Whilst Hamilton lies

The small medallion found at Chart Sutton by Mark Kirby. It must have belonged to John Cutts and bears the text of a psalm – coincidentally the very same scripture that appears almost alongside John's name on the Runnymede memorial.

buried in Folkestone (Hawkinge) Cemetery, we do know that Arthur Nicholls visited that crash site some time after the incident and found assorted pieces of clothing in the wreckage bearing linen tabs with Hamilton's name. Is it possible perhaps that partial remains were found and buried here? Possible perhaps that those remains, buried on the foreshore at Camber Castle where the Hurricane had crashed, were then re-buried as "unknown" at Northiam some time shortly afterwards?

And what of Camber itself? What connection with a possible missing RAF pilot do we have there? One intriguing possibility advanced by researcher John Ellis is that this might in fact be none other than the grave of Sgt Stanislav Duszynski who was killed in action on 11 September 1940. As we have seen, he is still missing but the crash location at Little Scotney is not more than one and a half miles from Camber. Is it possible that his unidentified remains were taken into Camber and buried on or near the beach – possibly by some unknown military unit? Of course, neither scenario may be linked to the Northiam burial at all and the airman could simply be an unknown flier who had been washed up on the beach from the English Channel. The fact of the matter is that we simply don't know, and probably never will. The clues are tantalisingly scant. Considering the possibilities is purely academic, although they provide an interesting exercise when attempting to arrive at answers and solutions. Without asking questions like these none of the cases in this book would have ever been solved.

If the Northiam case remains a puzzle then there is at least one other Battle of Britain casualty, originally buried as unknown, who must be covered here. That is the case of Sgt Geoffrey Pearson of 501 Squadron who had been shot down and killed on 6 September 1940. It was a case that was solved jointly by Winston Ramsey and Peter Cornwell, but based largely on the latter's research work.

Hurricane P3516 had been shot down over the Ashford area at around 0900hrs on 6 September 1940 with its pilot posted missing believed killed. He was Sgt G W Pearson, but although a body was found at the crash site on Cowleas Farm in Hothfield it could not be identified. Part of the problem was, no doubt, due to Geoffrey Pearson's superstition which persuaded him it was bad luck to carry his dog-tags. However, the rest of the case is best taken up in a joint letter submitted by Ramsey and Cornwell to Dept AR9(RAF) of the MOD, then the casualty branch:

"According to the records of No 49 Maintenance Unit who were responsible for inspection and salvage of crashed aircraft, Hurricane P3516 was inspected at Hothfield on 8 September 1940.

"The local ARP Warden at Hothfield when interviewed recalled the incident and volunteered the information that a dead Sergeant Pilot was recovered from the wreckage of this aircraft.

"Lympne Station Diary provides the following:

"10 September 1940 1710hrs. Unknown RAF pilot buried at Lympne. Killed in crash caused by enemy action 6 September 1940.

"It is noteworthy that Sergeant G W Pearson is the only Fighter Command casualty on 6 September 1940 unaccounted for – every other being buried in various cemeteries around the country.

"The Commonwealth War Graves Commission headstone confirms the date of death as 6 September 1940 which is most unusual in the case of an unknown pilot. Therefore, our contention is that the airman buried at St Stephen's Churchyard, Lympne, died through enemy action on 6 September 1940 and was a pilot according to the CWGC headstone. Therefore, it can only be Sgt G W Pearson of 501 Squadron who remains officially missing."

Just prior to Easter 1982, the MOD accepted the findings that this must indeed be the grave of Geoffrey Pearson and accordingly wrote to Pearson's family to say that they had duly instructed the CWGC to erect a new headstone bearing his name. Winston and Peter are therefore to be congratulated for their fine detective work that led to the case of yet another missing Battle of Britain pilot finally being solved. It is certainly always satisfying when work like this achieves such positive results. Bringing the missing Few back home does not always have to involve complex wreck recovery operations. Sometimes it is just a case of making sense of muddled records to throw light onto these mysteries. Sometimes though, and as we saw with the Northiam grave and as we shall see in the next chapters, making sense of the available information is not always so straightforward.

CHAPTER 15

I Regret to Inform You…

FOR THE family of every serviceman during World War Two the arrival of the Post Office telegram boy was a dreaded event. A portent that might well spell devastating news. Tersely worded, the impersonal scraps of paper the telegram boy delivered could convey monumental and utterly crushing information. In many cases they confirmed the death of a loved one and went on, matter-of-factly, to enquire about funeral arrangements. For all the world they were as impersonal and ordinary as if the telegram was merely asking about shopping arrangements.

For some though the telegram opened up years of uncertainty with notification that a loved one was "….reported missing due to air operations". As we have seen, that stark message had an awful effect on the next of kin who received such news. So

Flight Lieutenant W H Rhodes-Moorhouse DFC was also initially missing but his crash site was located by his mother and widow.

far in this book we have looked at cases where investigations, long after the event, have been instigated by third parties. Some families, however, refused to accept the classification of missing from the very outset and immediately started their own investigations as to what had happened to their loved ones. A case in point is Sgt Geoffrey Gilders who is dealt with in Chapter Eighteen but there were at least three other cases during the Battle of Britain where relatives set out to discover for themselves what had happened. Had they not done so there can be little doubt that these three pilots would have remained missing – at least, certainly for many years after the war.

Flt Lt William Rhodes-Moorhouse DFC was the very epitome of what many have thought a Battle of Britain pilot to be; dashing, handsome, courageous and breathtakingly glamorous. In the case of 'Willie' Rhodes-Moorhouse, he was also fabulously wealthy and well-connected. He also happened to be the son of Lt Rhodes-Moorhouse, the first air VC. Perhaps that wealth and all the social connections had earned him his place in 601 Squadron – popularly known as the 'Millionaires Squadron'. Either way, by the September of 1940 Willie was an experienced and seasoned fighter pilot having seen action in France and then the Battle of Britain. Between 18 May and 4 September, Rhodes-Moorhouse had shot down five enemy aircraft, shared in the destruction of four others and probably destroyed another four. The award of the Distinguished Flying Cross came on 30 July. Like many fighter pilots, however, he was overly superstitious and regarded the number eight as his lucky number. For that reason he chose Hurricane P8818 as 'his' aeroplane. The serial number had more eights than any other on the squadron! All his victories from 11 August onwards were claimed in this aircraft. It was also the aeroplane that would carry him to his death on 6 September 1940.

During an early morning engagement with Messerschmitt 109s over East Sussex and Kent 601 Squadron, airborne from Tangmere, had lost four pilots shot down around half past nine; Plt Off H T Gilbert, Fg Off Topolnicki, Flt Lt Davis and Flt Lt Rhodes-Moorhouse. Gilbert and Topolnicki were safe, Davis was dead and Rhodes-Moorhouse was missing, believed killed. Indeed, 'Missing believed killed' was the status reported to Willie's young wife, Amalia. It was, though, something that Amalia and Willie's mother, Linda, were unwilling to accept. Aware of the combat area in which 601 Squadron had been engaged, the pair set off for the Kent-Sussex border and canvassed local hospitals and police stations. Did anyone know anything? Were there reports of crashes that might be linked? Were there RAF casualties in local hospitals who were perhaps unconscious and unidentified and who might turn out to be Willie?

The clues were not long in coming and very soon the intrepid pair had news of two crashes – one near Hadlow Down in East Sussex and the other on a sewage treatment farm at High Brooms, Southborough – just on the outskirts of Royal Tunbridge Wells. Both had crashed at the right time on the morning of 6 September. However, what little remained above ground of the Hadlow Down crash had once been a Spitfire and not a Hurricane. Turning their attention to Southborough, the pair of ladies eventually found the unguarded crash site. It was just a crater in the soft ground not far from the High Brooms railway viaduct. Small boys had picked over the scattered debris and, to be frank, nothing substantial or particularly important remained to be seen. However, there was something small and *very* significant. Amalia picked up a torn piece of wood or metal on which was painted a partial serial number. Linda, William's mother, takes up the story:

"It [*the Hurricane*] was seen to dive suddenly out of control straight to earth from a great height. We went to where this had occurred to find only small pieces of the machine strewn round as it was completely buried in the soft earth. On one of the small pieces we found a number which was identified as the number of his 'plane. The number was 88 and strangely he had always believed 8 was his lucky number. Afterwards Sir Stephen [*his father-in-law, Sir Stephen Demetriadi*] arranged for the machine to be dug up and his body was found. He was cremated and his ashes eventually buried on top of the hill at Parnham where his father had been buried. His whole life had been vivid and, like a meteor, it ended before it was dimmed."

Under Sir Stephen's direction, army sappers dug out the wreckage with great difficulty – the family photograph album recording that William was finally extricated from a depth of twenty feet on Sunday 15 September – nine days after his loss. Without a doubt, and had it not been for the determination of both Linda and Amalia, the name of William Rhodes-Moorhouse DFC would surely have been added to those at Runnymede and he would probably have remained missing to this day. Today, the sewage farm is no more – it having being replaced by a local authority rubbish tip and now covered over by a huge landfill site. It would not, surely, have been a fitting place for the final repose of a Battle of Britain ace.

When Amalia and Linda had discounted and left the crash site at Howbourne Farm, near Hadlow Down, they could not have known that the family of its pilot were also engaged in a similar quest for a lost loved one. Pilot Officer William Gordon came from a well known distilling family and his kin travelled from Scotland to find news of their missing son who had been lost in 234 Squadron Spitfire – also on 6 September 1940. Whatever the trail was that led them to Howbourne Farm we cannot now be certain. However, suffice to say that it ultimately led to the realisation that their missing son was still trapped in the buried wreck of his Spitfire. By good fortune it turned out that civil

William Rhodes-Moorhouse's father-in-law Sir Stephen Demetriadi organised and supervised the operation to recover William's body near High Brooms, Tunbridge Wells.

Pilot Officer W H G Gordon was one of those pilots killed in action but for whom the location of the crash site and the casualty's body fell to the family to discover.

engineering contractors, Messrs Mowlems, were engaged on government work in the adjacent fields constructing anti-invasion measures such as pill boxes and tank traps. On site with them was a drag line excavator and the machine was quickly put to work extricating the wreckage. Sure enough, the sad remains of Bill 'Scotty' Gordon were extricated with the wreck of his aeroplane and he was ultimately laid to rest in the parish church at Mortlach in Banff, Scotland.

If the Rhodes-Moorhouse and Gordon families were perhaps able to pursue their tragic quests by virtue of their status and wealth, then such was not the case with Peter McIntosh. Peter had been born in South London and had lived and grown up in a middle-class family spending his formative years in Croydon where he attended Whitgift Middle School. His was not a life of privilege, private schools and country estates. Indeed, his working life had begun as a clerk with Eagle Star Insurance before he joined the RAFVR on 7 February 1939. Following the usual route of initial training and gaining his wings, Peter was posted to 151 Squadron on Hurricanes at North Weald and flew operationally with them during the Battle of Britain before his posting to another Hurricane unit, this time 605 'County of Warwick' Squadron at Croydon whom he joined on 13 October. It

Sgt Peter McIntosh.

must have been a pleasure for both Peter and his family for him to be back home in Croydon and able to spend time with friends and family. Sadly, that joy was shortlived.

On 12 October, Peter telephoned his parents to inform them that he was on ops that afternoon but would telephone them again during the evening to reassure them that he was all right. When no telephone call came Peter's father called the squadron to receive the devastating news that Peter was missing and had failed to return from an engagement with the enemy over the Kent coast. Nothing more was known. Undeterred, Peter's father and elder brother set out for the Kent coast and began to ask questions. It was not long before someone was found who had seen a Hurricane crash to earth following a dogfight at the same time Peter was last seen. Its pilot had not baled out and the family were directed to the spot alongside Littlestone Golf Course by a helpful farmer.

There, Peter's father found the crater and scattered debris usually left by aircraft that crashed in this manner and, nearby, he picked up part of the aircraft bearing the serial number P3022. Taking it home with him, Mr McIntosh telephoned the 605 Squadron adjutant; "Does the number P3022 mean anything?" Indeed it did. Hurricane P3022 was the aeroplane Peter had disappeared in. His father had literally stumbled across the crash site of Peter's aircraft, and he immediately pressed for its recovery although evidently had some difficulty in convincing the authorities to act and to find his son's body. Eventually, after some days, the sad task was finally carried out and it became possible for Peter to be buried in Shirley churchyard some ten days after his loss.

The cases of William Rhodes-Moorhouse, William Gordon and Peter McIntosh are all instances where families took the initiative to act and to find their loved ones. Had some of the other families affected by losses such as these acted similarly, especially where pilots had been shot down over their English homeland, then it is entirely likely that more of these hitherto missing airmen would have been accounted for long ago. We have to look no further than the cases of Brimble, Cutts, Rushmer, Scott and Shaw, for example, to realise how different the endings of those stories in 1940 might well have been.

16 Still Missing

Sgt Derrick Halton of 615 Squadron and his wife, Margaret. Halton was shot down and posted missing presumed killed on 15 August 1940. Suggestions that he may have crashed at Seal, near Sevenoaks, are probably incorrect. It is likely that he crashed into the sea somewhere in the Folkestone area. He is still missing.

A S WE have read in earlier chapters, the research during the 1970s to fill in the detail of who shot down who, as well as when and where, was groundbreaking work. Prominent amongst those who helped complete our knowledge of the minutiae of the battles in 1940 were, *inter alia*, Peter Foote, Alan Brown, Denis Knight and Peter Cornwell. It was Cornwell who compiled the masterful listings of all known RAF and Luftwaffe losses during the Battle of Britain that would later be published in the definitive

Battle of Britain Then & Now. Based upon contemporary material and input from almost countless sources, the listings also relied upon assessments from established researchers and amateur historians alike – including the growing numbers of those involved in aviation archaeology. The latter group had often found tangible evidence enabling specific aircraft and their particular fates to be identified and thus fill in missing details. As such they were an invaluable source.

That said, of course, the completed data could not always be relied upon as absolutely accurate. Errors in original documentation and records and the fact that a 'best-guess' sometimes had to be judiciously applied to the detail of certain crashes, meant that the loss lists were almost a work in progress. The reprinting of the book in no less than five up-dated versions bears testimony to this, and this was not least of all due to the fact that readers often willingly and helpfully wrote in with fresh information, corrections and additions. One case that emerged out of the comprehensive loss listings for the battle was that of Sgt Derrick Halton of 615 Squadron, shot down on 15 August 1940.

With published sources giving the location of the crash of Sgt Halton's Hurricane as Seal, near Sevenoaks, a considerable degree of searching and researching by local enthusiasts ensued in what were ultimately futile attempts to tie down further the possible crash site. Eventually, a former schoolboy who had been evacuated with his school to Stonepitts House, Seal, told how he recalled what he had thought to have been a Hurricane crashing vertically into fields below the house that had been commandeered by the school. He was adamant that the incident was during the Battle of Britain, and possibly during August. He couldn't be sure though. Although the evidence was circumstantial it wasn't long before a tenuous link was being established with Derrick Halton, but searches in the fields below Stonepits indicated no obvious trace of an aircraft having crashed there. The trail went cold.

Although nothing further had come to light to link Halton to any crash at Seal the question remained; if his Hurricane *had* crashed at Seal, then where was it? And *where* had the information about a crash at Seal originated in the first place? Local contemporary records revealed nothing that pointed to an incident here on 15 August 1940 – so what did the operations record book for 615 Squadron record for the day? Perhaps, even if indirectly, the clue was there after all. Under "Summary of Events" the 615 Squadron ORB states:

> "In the morning the Squadron patrolled near Dungeness. "A" Flight saw nothing but Spitfires but "B" Flight were attacked by six Me 109's diving out of the sun. Pilot Officer Truran received one cannon shell in fuselage which caught alight but fortunately went out and one shell in the wing near petrol tank. He managed to land machine safely at Kenley in spite of shrapnel wounds in his leg. Flying Officer Eyre and Pilot Officer Lofts brought down the Me 109 which had attacked Pilot Officer Truran. The aircraft dived in flames near Folkestone. Pilot Officer Evans landed at Hawkinge with bullet holes through glycol tank. Sgt Halton is missing."

There is, of course, no doubting that the battle in which 615 Squadron found itself involved around mid-day on 15 August 1940 was over the coastal area of Folkestone. In that context there are two points that must be considered. First, it is unlikely that Halton would have

SHIRE EVENING TELEGRAPH, W

S HURRICANE PILOT MISSING.

Former Member of "Evening Telegraph" Staff.

LAST seen diving through a bank of clouds, 15,000 feet above sea level, his "Hurricane" riddled with bullets from German Messerschmitts, a former "Evening Telegraph" reporter has been reported missing.

He is Sergt. Pilot Derrick Halton, aged 21 years, who was on our staff at Rushden and Kettering several years ago. Last September he married a Rushden girl, Miss

SERGT-PILOT HALTON.

Margaret (Peggy) Mather, of the "Old Rectory," and since their marriage his wife has been living close to the aerodromes at which he was stationed.

At dawn last Thursday, Sergt Pilot Halton took off with his squadron, and intercepted waves of Nazi planes which were coming over the Channel. In the thick of the fight, two of his friends saw him being fiercely attacked by two Messerschmitts They went to his aid and attacked the Germans, but by then his crippled "Hurricane" was plunging through a bank of clouds below.

The Air Ministry have pointed out to Mrs. Halton that he may have crashed in German-occupied territory or been picked up by a German patrol boat.

The missing pilot, who was a free-lance journalist in London before the war, joined the R.A.F Volunteer Reserve in April of last year and took his "wings" last March, when he went on active service

One of his brothers, John, who was a Grimsby journalist before the war and began his career on the "Evening Telegraph" staff at Rushden, is also serving in the Royal Air Force, and the other brother, Joe, is a sub-lieutenant in the Navy. His father, Mr J W Halton, is head dispenser at Northampton General Hospital.

The newspaper clipping that refers to the combat in which Sgt Halton was lost taking place over a coastal area.

been physically shot down over Seal given that this is some fifty miles from where the action had been centred. Of course, one cannot exclude the possibility that he crashed at Seal whilst attempting to return, perhaps with a damaged aircraft or wounded, to his Kenley base. Secondly, given that the action was over Folkestone then it will be noted this is remarkably close to Deal. Deal? Seal? Could the two have been somehow confused? Whilst this is speculation without any firm evidential basis, it is difficult to make any sense of the reports about a crash at Seal. Fortunately we have a report from the 21 August 1940 edition of the *Northamptonshire Evening Telegraph* to help us a little further. In its columns one can find a published notice about one of that newspaper's former members of staff. Under "Hurricane Pilot Missing" was printed the following narrative: "Last seen diving through a bank of clouds, 15,000ft above sea level, his Hurricane riddled with bullets from a German Messerschmitt a former *Evening Telegraph* reporter has been reported missing."

The report goes on:

"….last Thursday Sgt Pilot Halton took off with his squadron and intercepted waves of Nazi planes which were coming over the Channel. In the thick of the fight two of his friends saw him being fiercely attacked by two Messerschmitts. They went to his aid and attacked the Germans, but by then his crippled Hurricane was plunging through a bank of clouds below. The Air Ministry have pointed out to Mrs Halton that he may have crashed in German territory or been picked up by a German patrol boat."

There exists no particular reason to doubt this contemporary report and it seems reasonable to conclude that Sgt Halton crashed into the English Channel with his Hurricane, P2801. Equally, there seems to exist no evidence to link Sgt Halton with a crash at Seal. And the Hurricane that the young schoolboy had seen crash to earth? Most probably this was Sgt Jack Hammerton's Hurricane that crashed, fatally, at Noah's Ark, Kemsing, on 6 November 1940 in an episode wholly unrelated to the loss of Derrick Halton.

When Sgt Pilot Halton failed to return that day the squadron adjutant had the terrible task of telling Margaret, his wife of less than one year, that he was missing. He didn't have far to travel in order to tell her. Their marital home was at Fulford Road in Caterham Hill – just a stone's throw from RAF Kenley. Her grief must have been compounded on a daily basis as Hurricanes flew over, to and from the airfield, while all hope for his survival rapidly ebbed away.

Sgt Derrick Halton is one of The Few who remains missing in action.

CHAPTER 17

Those Left Behind

READERS OF this book might well ask the question: are there other pilots missing from the Battle of Britain whose whereabouts are known or suspected but who have not yet been recovered? The answer is yes.

Denzil Bacon was eleven years old when he stood on the quay at Burnham-on-Crouch on the Essex coast with two other boys and watched an air battle develop overhead. It was 3 September 1940 at about half past ten in the morning when suddenly a Hurricane wobbled out of the fight overhead and came flying along the River Crouch. The boys remarked at its gyrations as it soared and dived, flipped onto its back, righted itself and veered this way and that. Thinking about it in later years, Denzil would describe it as being as if the pilot was drunk. Suddenly it was all over and the Hurricane plunged vertically into the river at Redward Creek. The tide was in and the aeroplane vanished from sight. Nobody had got out.

The boat owners at Burnham, Messrs Pettigrews, sent out a boat but there was nothing that could be done. Returning to the quay, the boatman had pulled up a large piece of the tail section which was displayed on the quay to raise money for the Spitfire fund under a sign that said: "Help Replace

Sgt Gerald Edworthy of 46 Squadron was shot down in his Hurricane over Essex during the morning of 3 September 1940. There can be no doubting that he crashed with his Hurricane onto the north shore of the River Crouch near Burnham-on-Crouch, close to Redward Creek. Essex ARP control reported: "3/9/1940 10.30hrs Aircraft crashed into River Crouch two miles below Burnham" then a follow-up report stated: "Believed Spitfire (sic) Redward Creek. Completely disappeared. Military watching".

This clearly relates to the loss of Sgt Gerald Edworthy although the Ministry of Defence are dismissive of the evidence linking the crash to this pilot and query the accuracy of ARP reports such as this one. In the view of the author this is an open and shut case. Sgt Edworthy certainly crashed at Redward Creek.

This One!" When the tide had gone out just an imprint on the glutinous mud and a few scattered bits of debris marked the spot. A few more tides and all the evidence had gone. Even venturing onto the deep black mud is hazardous and everyone knew or believed that the pilot had gone forever. Little thought was ever given locally as to who he might have been.

In 1981, when the author looked at reports of the loss, it again seemed that it was possible to name the pilot. Given that the date was known there really could only be one possibility. This had been Hurricane P3064 flown by Sgt Gerald Edworthy. Whilst salvage seemed unlikely it was a case, really, of never say never and in May 1981 Steve Vizard and the author struggled out across the mud to search. Surprisingly a considerable amount of aircraft debris was strewn around and all of it identifiable as Hurricane. The exact position of the impact, though, was impossible at that stage to determine but it was felt that the matter should be brought to the attention of Edworthy's family if they could be found.

Following the usual lines of enquiry, Gerald's half-brother and half-sister were traced to the west country and apprised of the situation. Stunned to discover the information about Gerald both were keen that attempts should be made to find him, although it was explained that this might be exceedingly difficult given the conditions at the site. Under the circumstances it was felt that the Edworthy family would be best to contact the MOD to see if any official help might be available. With huge military resources at their disposal any attempt at recovery *might* stand a better chance than if carried out by a team of volunteers armed with buckets and spades.

Unfortunately, when the case was put to the MOD the response was far from encouraging. Mr Tom Webb was then head of Dept AR9(RAF), the service casualty branch and wrote to the family on 26 January 1982:

"We have studied the RAF casualty records most thoroughly and regrettably we are unable to determine the position where your brother's aircraft crashed, nor does our investigation of the records of 46 Squadron, of which your brother was a member, reveal any further evidence of significance. The squadron, whilst on patrol, intercepted a formation of eighty enemy aircraft just north of Southend and your brother was missing from this action. No other details are available from the archives.

"Detailed research by aviation enthusiasts among local records and other sources often reveals further information concerning wartime aircraft crashes but their conclusions do not always prove reliable. Contemporary ARP reports, for example, are often suspect and eye witness accounts re-told forty years later are rarely accurate."

The letter went on to explain that no further action could be taken by the MOD in this matter and that they did not accept the identity of this crash site as being Sgt Gerald Edworthy's Hurricane. All in all it was a disappointing and puzzling reply. The evidence was there from local reports that indicated this could only involve Sgt Edworthy and yet the authorities were dismissive of this notion. Discrediting both contemporary records and eye witness accounts as "unreliable" or "seldom accurate" was hardly fair given the not infrequent failings or short-comings in the ministry's own reports!

Gerald's proud parents carefully preserved this clipping from *Illustrated* of 18 May 1940 in which their son appears centre back. It was a cherished memento of their boy although they were denied the chance of ever knowing what had become of him.

Certainly, each report from whatever source needed to be looked at in context and weighed carefully against other established facts. In the case of the Redward Creek Hurricane crash however, the author feels that the MOD made an inappropriate judgement. The result has been that Sgt Edworthy's relatives were never given the chance to draw any conclusion to their brother's loss. Maybe, one day, the case will be looked at again and with the passage of time and the development of new machinery and technology, it will perhaps become possible to locate and recover easily Sgt Edworthy from his Hurricane in the River Crouch. Sadly, if that day should ever come, it will most likely be long after all those who knew Gerald and who care about him have gone.

Of other cases, there are two that merit discussion. The first is another Hurricane lost in coastal and tidal mud on the east coast and not terribly far from the place of Gerald Edworthy's loss. On 31 August 1940 a British fighter was seen to crash at Osea Island in the River Blackwater and the event was recorded in the Essex County Council war diary: "Crashed aircraft report. British Spitfire [sic] found West Point, Osea Island, pilot believed drowned at 0845hrs." Later, there is further clarification: "Plane now identified as V7373, confirmed pilot drowned."

Returning to the point made above about the accuracy of contemporary reports, we have here some very interesting evidence. It is a case, though, of interpretation rather than taking what we read at face value. V7373 was, as it happens, a Hurricane but the problem here is that it survived the Battle of Britain. On the other hand, Hurricane **V7378** was a Hurricane lost in this very area on 31 August 1940 and at *exactly* the time given in the reports. A Spitfire could be discounted and the mis-reading of the final digit of a three for an eight could be easily explained as either a simple transcription error or difficulty in reading the number accurately on crumpled and possibly submerged wreckage. So much for the MOD's dismissal of local and contemporary reports.

In this case, interpretation of these local records enables us to identify this particular wreck as the Hurricane flown by Flt Lt P S Weaver DFC of 56 Squadron. 'Percy' Weaver is still missing and the MOD records, apparently, give no indication as to exactly where he fell. A sock bearing a linen tab with the name WEAVER was evidently found nearby – the only evidence the family ever had in relation to his loss. Surviving family members would certainly like Percy found and brought home. Legal restraints and site conditions make that, perhaps, rather unlikely. Maybe one day he will be laid to rest – and using the clues established from local ARP reports of which the MOD have been so scathingly dismissive.

The final case, another Hurricane pilot, has rather less about it in the way of clues and what we do have is largely circumstantial. On 11 September 1940 and in the same battle that Sgt Duszynski was lost Flt Lt D P Hughes, also of Duszynski's 238 Squadron, was shot down in Hurricane V7240 and posted missing. Local researcher and former Brenzett Aeronautical Museum member John Elgar-Whinney had found an original but rather tatty ARP map based on the Lydd area. On it were marked all aircraft losses in the district and a check for accuracy of those sites that have since been established (eg by subsequent excavation) proved its reliability.

The crash site was marked accurately for Sgt Duszynski, but just a short distance away was marked another crash on the same day. Hughes had been lost in the same combat, although other reports suggest the area of his loss to be Brooklands. If that was meant to be Brooklands in Surrey then this is many miles away to the north west and nowhere near the scene of the action that day. However, just a few miles distant from the mark on the map is the tiny village of Brookland. Brooklands? Brookland? It is largely just supposition though, and in this instance the MOD might rightly query any conclusion that is reached to place Flt Lt Hughes in this location.

There can be little doubting what happened to Sgt Edworthy or to Flt Lt Weaver. The case for Flt Lt Hughes is less convincing although it would be interesting to know what is held on file in the RAF casualty report for this pilot. It may yet be many more years before those files appear in the public domain. Until then we have only the jig-saw assembly of reports from other sources to rely upon. As we have seen, and despite the misgivings of the Ministry of Defence, they have thus far served well the purpose of finding and identifying missing casualties from the Battle of Britain.

CHAPTER 18

"No Trace of Him Could Be Found…"

J OHN GILDERS was a Battle of Britain survivor. Not a casualty of the battle *per se* but all the same one whose story very much deserves to be told here. Like all of the previous chapters charting other cases, this too is a surprising story. Quite possibly Sgt John Stanley Gilders will be the last of Churchill's missing few to have their names ultimately removed from the Runnymede Memorial. That he was ever missing in the first place is truly extraordinary.

John Gilders was born in Deal, Kent, on 4 October 1919 the son of John and Ivy Gilders. John's father, an accountant, worked for the Unilever Company in Brazil where the young John spent his early childhood before the family returned home to England, where John completed his education at Bancroft School at Woodford Green in Essex where he achieved creditable passes in his school certificate exams. On 21 May 1938 he commenced his air force career at 18 Elementary & Reserve Flying Training School, Woking. Here, he began his flying training on a Tiger Moth and had progressed sufficiently to make his first solo flight in Tiger Moth K4291 on 11 June 1938. From 18 ERFTS John moved on to 1 Initial Training Wing,

Sgt Pilot John Gilders of 41 Squadron stands in time-honoured traditional fighter pilot pose in front of Spitfire EB-J. He vanished on 21 February 1941 although the RAF knew exactly where he had crashed and advised the family accordingly.

John's father George Gilders campaigned tirelessly to discover what had become of his son, and was disbelieving of the information he was being fed, suspecting there had been a cover-up. As events turned out his suspicions were well founded. Father and son are photographed here at their Surrey home.

Cambridge, and thence to 3 Service Flying Training School at South Cerney in February 1940. On 15 June 1940 he was given his first operational posting: 72 Squadron at RAF Acklington.

John received extensive training on the unit's Magister, then a Harvard, before being let loose on one of the squadron's Spitfires for the first time on 26 June when he flew K9958 for one hour and thirty-five minutes. At the start of the Battle of Britain the squadron moved south to Biggin Hill on 31 August, although John flew down as a passenger in Handley Page Harrow K7000 as the result of minor injuries sustained during a night landing

A line up of 41 Squadron pilots at RAF Hornchurch during early 1941. John stands third from right. Fifth from right is the CO, Sqn Ldr D O Finlay, who tried hard to get 'Gilly' Gilders found.

accident in Spitfire N3221 when the aircraft had finished up on its back in a field next to the aerodrome. He had been lucky to survive.

No sooner had the squadron arrived in Kent than it was thrown into action, John flying two interception patrols on 1 September. The next day he hit and damaged a Dornier 17 but was set upon by two Me 109s before he could finish off the bomber. On the 4th he claimed a Messerschmitt 110 shot down in flames, but the following day would be a bad one for the squadron. Two of its pilots were shot down and killed and a third wounded. John managed to limp back to RAF Croydon in Spitfire R6777 where no less than thirty-five bullet holes were counted in his aircraft. It had been another lucky escape.

Nevertheless, his flying career was to continue with further claims being made by Gilders on 10 September when he shared a Dornier 215 (sic) with Plt Off Robson. A Me 109 was shot down near Cranbrook on the 11th and a Heinkel 111 forced down on the 15th. On the 27th, 18,000ft above Sevenoaks, the squadron met a mixed formation of Junkers 88s and Messerschmitt 109s, whereupon John shot a wing off one of the Messerschmitts

Sgt Bob Beardsley of 41 Squadron saw John Gilders dive away from the formation and vanish. With other pilots he followed him down and called him up vainly over the radio before having to pull out of the dive to avoid over stressing his aircraft.

and sent another enemy aircraft, one of the bombers, crashing to earth. October saw no let up with further skirmishes but no claims, although on the 9th of that month he yet again returned home with his Spitfire badly shot up.

By the time the squadron had moved north to the relative quiet backwater of Leconfield on 19 October he was a seasoned veteran of air fighting. As an experienced NCO pilot he was posted to 616 Squadron at Kirton-in-Lindsay on 10 November although it was to be a short stay and by 26th of that month he had again been posted south, this time to join 41 Squadron at RAF Hornchurch.

Led by pre-war Olympic hurdler Sqn Ldr Donald Finlay, 41 Squadron was a battle-hardened outfit and John undoubtedly felt at ease and at home here amongst a nucleus of experienced combat fliers. However, with a comparative lull in daytime activity over Britain by the Luftwaffe, John's flying was almost exclusively confined to routine patrols and he completed no less than twenty-three such sorties during his time with 41 Squadron. This monotony of routine patrols was broken by two flights on 5 February 1941 when he participated in offensive patrols to St Omer and Ostend in what was RAF Fighter Command's newly aggressive strategy of taking the war directly to the enemy. The overall monotony of service life, however, was broken by the respite of some brief leave at home during early February when he became engaged to be married to Miss Molly Nicholson.

However, the joy was short lived and it was during just another one of the squadron's routine patrols on 21 February 1941 that Sgt John Gilders failed to return.

Exactly what occurred on that flight remains a mystery and very few clues have really come to light to establish the reason for his loss. There are no Luftwaffe fighter claims for action over the UK that day and available evidence tends to indicate that John's disappearance was due to anoxia, more simply described as oxygen starvation. Of all the casualties detailed in this volume, John Gilders is the only one who can definitely be attributed to a non-combat related cause.

At 1210hrs on 21 February 1941, six aircraft of 41 Squadron were ordered off from Hornchurch and led by Flt Lt John McKenzie in P7730. The remaining five aircraft and pilots were: Plt Off Briggs (P7610), Plt Off Ford (P7508), Sgt Beardsley (P7689), Sgt Hopkinson (P7371) and Sgt Gilders (P7816). The details of the flight, albeit brief, are recorded in the 41 Squadron operations record book:

"Six aircraft ordered to patrol Ramsgate, Canterbury and Dungeness. Plt Off Ford leading the top pair did not see Sgt Gilders who should have kept with him. Sgt Hopkinson reports that he saw a Spitfire doing a steep climbing turn below and then shoot away. He turned and saw the aircraft disappear through the haze at 20-25,000ft. This occurred off Folkestone – the aircraft, presumably Sgt Gilders, being in a gentle dive. Two bandits were reported and searched for but appear to have been on the French coast. Patrol landed Hornchurch 1405hrs."

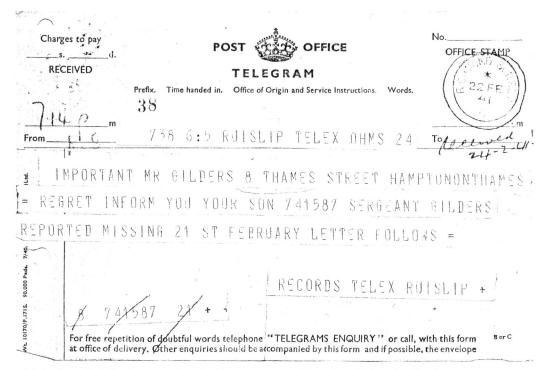

This is the official telegram, dreaded by so many, telling the Gilders family their son was missing.

Although offering no real insight into the fate of Spitfire P7816 or John Gilders, other information was to come to light in 1941 that clearly indicated the fate of both aeroplane and pilot. More detail has also come from one of the other pilots on that fateful patrol. Sgt R A Beardsley, now Sqn Ldr Beardsley, wrote in November 1987:

"John 'Gilly' Gilders' death was, as far as my memory goes, a tragic accident. The previous day's sortie over the Channel had been bounced by the new Me 109Fs and we lost two pilots, Sgts McAdam and Angus. During the next sortie on 21 February we failed to make contact with the Luftwaffe and were at 32,000ft and just letting down to a lower altitude when John's aircraft pulled up in a turn and then dived steeply. He was called-up frequently over the R/T but failed to answer and whilst we followed him down we could not keep up without over stressing our aircraft and had to pull out. On arrival back at Hornchurch we were told that the aircraft had gone in vertically and the engine was buried deep. The report suggested anoxia as a result of the very high altitude and that he had passed out and not recovered. In those days the oxygen control was a simple butterfly and I had once completely unwound my own at extreme altitude and had it come off in my hand!"

Two other pilots of 41 Squadron had been shot down and killed the previous day; Sgts McAdam and Angus. Here, Sgt John McAdam sits astride his Spitfire EB-A. When McAdam was recovered from the sea there was some confusion that it might be John Gilders and this resulted in the Gilders family being told, initially, that their son had been found and his body was at Hawkinge.

Bob Beardsley's account, although written some forty-six years after the event, at least clears up the airborne details of 21 February 1941 although the circumstances of the actual crash itself and of subsequent events have proved rather more difficult to unravel. As soon as John Gilders failed to return, a chain of events was placed in motion that caused much official confusion and great distress to the family. It was to continue with varying repercussions that were felt right up until the 1990s, and that had begun with the delivery of the dreaded telegram to the Gilders family in Hampton-on-Thames to notify them that Sgt Gilders was missing.

Sgt R A Angus was the other pilot shot down over the Dover-Folkestone area with McAdam. Sgt Angus was never found and is still classified as missing.

John's loss came at a time of administrative upheaval for 41 Squadron as the unit prepared for a move northwards to RAF Catterick on 23 February. The chaos of preparations to move may well have had some bearing on subsequent events, although Fg Off D A Adams recalled vividly the aftermath of 'Gilly' Gilders' disappearance and that the CO, Sqn Ldr Finlay, dashed off to the crash site in a staff car in order to try and organise the retrieval of his body. It was ultimately a futile effort. Another factor in the dreadful shambles that caused the Gilders family and John's fiancé so much grief would be 41 Squadron's loss of two other sergeant pilots the day before.

When Sgts McAdam and Angus were shot down over Dover on 20 February, only the body of Ulsterman McAdam was recovered from the sea. Angus was never found. Taken to nearby RAF Hawkinge, McAdam was sent home for burial in Northern Ireland but, somehow, this had resulted in the Gilders family being notified on 27 February that it was their son's body that had been found and he was now at Hawkinge. It was only the start of a long and dreadful shambles. Whilst the circumstances of John's loss against a background of general fog of war might well explain the confusion that resulted, this did little to allay the pain of the family and George embarked upon a long campaign of letter writing in an effort to establish what had happened to his son. Getting at the truth proved hugely difficult, and the answers George Gilders finally got were actually a very long way from how things really were.

Although the RAF had quickly established that Spitfire P7816 had crashed and buried itself in a meadow alongside the River Stour at Chilham, near Canterbury, there was evidently no trace of John. Unusually, the Air Ministry were able to tell Mr Gilders where his son's aeroplane had fallen. It went on to tell him that no trace of John could be found there and offered various scenarios to explain why Sgt Gilders could not be located.

Tel. No. Holborn 3434.

Ext....................

P.357402/41.

AIR MINISTRY. Dept.Q.J.

ADASTRAL HOUSE,

KINGSWAY, W.C.2.

24ᵗʰ March, 1941.

Dear Mr Gilders,

I am writing to confirm the information given you on your
visit here to-day about what we had been able to find out concerning
the very regrettable loss of your son's aircraft on 21st February.

The officer from No.49 Maintenance Unit who actually
supervised the salvage of the aircraft, Spitfire P.7816, stated it
had crashed near Chilham, close to the main Ashford-Canterbury road,
in a very soft and wet patch of ground.

The aircraft had exploded on impact and the engine was
buried in a hole some 16 feet deep which was full of water. The
pieces of the aircraft covered a large area and these were all
collected and the aircraft identified from it's number P.7816.

Although pieces of the cockpit and centre section were
collected no trace could be found of the pilot, his clothing, or
parachute. Owing to the soft nature of the ground it took all day
to dig out the engine and the officer concerned is convinced the
pilot was not in the wreckage.

Furthermore a policeman who saw the aircraft crash told the
officer it came down out of control and that no pilot was in it.

The most unfortunate mistake over your son being reported
killed was due to confusion over two crashes which occurred the same
day in that vicinity, and a pilot being found in the wreckage of the
other aircraft.

The Police at Chilham were then asked whether any report
had reached them of a pilot having descended by parachute on that
date. The Inspector stated the district was an agricultural

/ one

G.G. Gilders, Esq.,
    8, Thames Street,
        Hampton-on-Thames,
            Middlesex.

George Gilders continued to be unhappy about what he was being told and eventually
journeyed down to RAF Faygate to interview the 49 Maintenance Unit officer who had been
responsible for overseeing the recovery of John's aeroplane. What he found out had left him
feeling no less reassured. Quite simply, he felt uneasy about the account he had consistently

one, fairly thickly populated and no such report had yet reached
him. He also remembered the crash on 21st February.

We then asked the Chief Constable of Kent's office at
Maidstone to enquire from all the County Police offices in the
area whether any traces had been found of the pilot. I am very
much afraid he could only obtain negative information from all
his enquiries and was sure if any parachute descent had been made
on land the pilot or his parachute would have been found by now.

We find that reports from fighter squadrons rarely are
able to throw any light on what happens to aircraft that are missing,
after contact has been made with the enemy, as all pilots in the
various sections are intent on their own battles and rarely notice
what is happening to other pilots during combat.

From the information we have collected it is only possible
to assume that your son baled out, due to his aircraft having been
damaged by enemy action and he was blown out to sea. We have asked
the Meteorological Office for the weather report over that part of
Kent on 21st February and here it is :-

Wind North West at 12.15 hours.
on   surface   15 - 20 miles per hour
at   2,000 feet   30   "   "   "
at   10,000 feet   .50   "   "   "

Chilham is some 15 miles from the coast in a N.W. direction
so had he baled out somewhere in that vicinity at 10,000 feet or over,
the wind was in sufficient force to have blown him out to sea.

I do wish we had a more encouraging report to send you after
the long suspense you and Mrs. Gilders have been suffering, but perhaps
it will be some consolation for you to know the facts we have been
able to collect, which I'm afraid look rather formal and callous when
put down on paper. But please realise how much we sympathise with
you in your anxiety.

Yours sincerely.

R.H.Walsh

John Gilders' father became impatient and mistrustful of the information being given to him
by the Air Ministry about his missing son. Here, on this long explanatory letter, he has clearly
shown his dissatisfaction – pencilling in his various doubts and concerns and underlining key
points that he queried or questioned. Mr Gilders sensed he was not being told the whole
truth. In fact, he was told incorrectly that the engine of his son's aeroplane had been dug out
from sixteen feet and there was no trace of John. As events would show many years later this
was simply not true.

been given by the RAF. He had every reason to be uneasy. Picking up the statement by R H
Walsh in the 24 March letter relating to the observations of the local policeman, Mr Gilders
eventually wrote to the Chief Constable of Kent, J A Davison. Davison's reply on 25 August
1941 was unequivocal:

"It is the opinion of the Police Officer who saw the 'plane prior to the crash that the pilot was in it, but I don't think the information I have received establishes clearly that this was so."

It was directly at variance with what Walsh at the Air Ministry had told Mr Gilders about the opinion of the local police. Furthermore, it made no reference to the subsequent recovery that the Air Ministry were claiming had been carried out although it is reasonable to assume that the police *would* most certainly have been aware of any such extensive salvage operations. Davison went on:

"The crash was followed by a fire but not the intense fire usually associated with a burning aircraft and half an hour after the crash the fire was negligible. In the opinion of the local Police Sergeant it is not reasonable to believe that all traces of the pilot and parachute would be consumed by the fire."

Even more astonishing was a further letter from Davison on 9 September 1941 to George Gilders. In it, Davison wrote:

"As you already know from the Air Ministry your son's body has not yet been recovered from his 'plane and I do understand the distress this must be causing you. I sincerely hope that it will be possible to recover his remains in the fullness of time."

In fact, and as we have already seen, the Air Ministry had previously stated that the recovery of John's body was impossible. Indeed, they had been absolutely adamant it wasn't there. At best there had been some dreadful confusion. At worst, George Gilders had been lied to – and all available evidence points strongly to the latter.

During 1971 it was Tony Graves and John Tickner of the London Air Museum who picked matters up again in the case of Sgt Gilders. Visiting the crash site, the pair found a broken wire hawser going down into the ground. It was immovable and clearly attached to something heavy buried much deeper. Round and about there was the usual detritus associated with aircraft crashes of this nature – shards of alloy, bullet cases and pieces of perspex. However, and whilst the site of Sgt Gilders's crash had clearly been located, the landowner was unwilling to allow any excavations there. It was almost as if the farmer was merely continuing a cover-up that George Gilders had suspected some thirty years earlier. As if to reinforce the unfortunate treatment consistently meted out to the Gilders family, the landowner had one more insult to throw at them. On Remembrance Sunday 1987 John's brother Geoffrey made a pilgrimage to the crash site to place a wreath of poppies there. The farmer was unmoved. Nobody was going to walk across his land whoever they were. The wreath had to be left in a roadside hedge.

In the following years, enthusiast Dick Walker took up the Gilders case. Would it not be possible, Dick reasoned, for the MOD to force the landowner to allow official access to the site for further investigations? He wrote to them to ask. The reply, when it came, was unhelpful. Ironically, the Protection of Military Remains Act prevents a landowner from recovering a buried aircraft on his land without a licence but does not provide the MOD

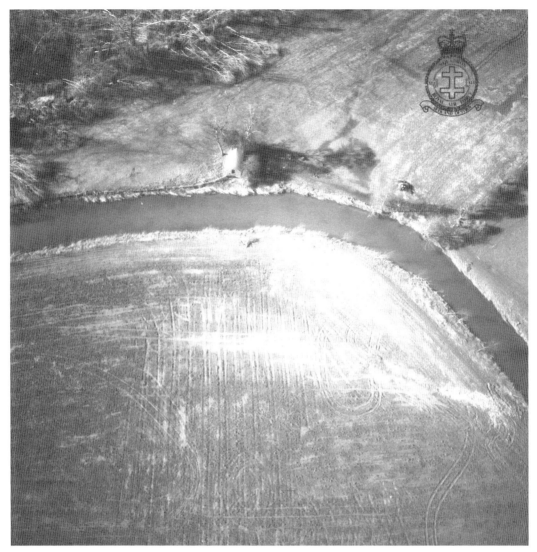

During the early 1980s an RAF Jaguar from 41 Squadron, Coltishall, made a low pass over the site at Chilham in salute and took this photograph. The crash site is on the nearest side of the river bank, just opposite the small building.

with the right to enter the site and recover an aircraft or pilot. In such cases, and even where the Crown claimed title, the Crown's representatives would require the landowner's consent. If this were not forthcoming then the legal position would be what is known as "the tort of conversion". In other words, a denial of the Crown's claim of title to the aircraft. Even supposing the landowner *would* allow access to the site, the MOD had no intention of making a recovery attempt. Equally, they would not grant a licence for private recovery either. Catch 22 again.

By 1994, Mark Kirby had already made something of a name for himself as a champion for the cause of missing aircrew and it was not long before his attention had turned to Chilham and Sgt Gilders. By now, the previous landowner had left and the new occupant was amenable to the idea of excavation and recovery. Indeed, he was shocked to discover

The same scene at ground level on 20 April 1994 when the recovery of John Gilders's Spitfire got underway.

that a grim secret may well lie beneath his pasture. There was, of course, the small problem of obtaining a licence for recovery from the MOD and it was already certain that no such licence would ever be forthcoming.

However, Mark was not to be deterred. He discussed the matter with John's surviving brother and sister, Geoffrey and Margaret, and ascertained that their wishes had remained unchanged from those expressed so long ago by their late father; whatever was left of John should be recovered. At least, the site must be properly investigated. Mark was prepared to take the consequences and to do what he considered to be the right thing by John Gilders, John's late father and the surviving siblings. In any event, there were clearly question marks hanging over what might still be there – especially given the Air Ministry correspondence from 1941. Maybe something would be found that would somehow solve the mystery of John's disappearance? In an emotional conversation with Mark, John's sister Margaret Lawson told him: "Look after John." He told her he would. It was a promise that he was determined to keep, and on 20 April 1994 Mark mounted a full-scale recovery operation at Chilham. What he found there was surprising to say the very least.

At a little over two feet beneath the surface of the field, the remains of John Gilders and his parachute were found in the wreckage of the cockpit. It was barely below the plough-line. The force of the impact had compressed what was left of the fuselage into the back of the Rolls-Royce Merlin engine and the front of the engine itself was no more than seven or eight feet into the ground. This was the engine and cockpit that the RAF maintenance unit had claimed they excavated at this very site from a depth of sixteen feet. It was also the body of the pilot they had said was not there. It was the parachute they suggested might have taken John out across the English Channel.

All along, John had lain there just yards from a busy main road. Recovery in 1941 would have been a very simple matter indeed. Instead, George and the family had been left not knowing and wondering where their son was. It was unforgivable. Angered however by the unlicenced recovery that had thrown up yet another missing casualty to deal with, and by the cringing embarrassment that the recovery would now cause, the MOD pressed the local police to prosecute Mark Kirby and he was duly arrested and charged with offences under the Protection of Military Remains Act. Six months later Mark was summonsed to appear before the local magistrates court.

In presenting his case to the Justices, Mark pleaded guilty to the charges laid against him. After all, it was an "absolute offence" and he could hardly claim that he did have an MOD licence! However, he relied not only upon evidence that he was acting in accordance with the wishes of the family but by the submission of the 1941 correspondence from the Air Ministry to the Gilders family as mitigation for the offence with which he had been charged. The magistrates were clearly impressed by Mark's case and by the mendacious nature of the now historic Air Ministry letters. The case was thrown out and Mark Kirby was granted an absolute discharge.

Incredibly, the engine the RAF claimed had been dug out from sixteen feet in 1941 was found just below the surface of the field at Chilham. The back of the Rolls-Royce Merlin can be seen here in the left foreground of the excavation. John Gilders was found with the engine just below the topsoil.

On 5 December 1994 the district's coroner, Brian Smith, held a formal inquest into the case of Sgt Gilders where he was formally named and identified and a verdict of "Died on War Service" entered. Mr Smith was not in any way critical of the recovery that had taken place and paid homage to John Gilders by appearing in court in full wig and gown. He explained that it was not normal practice for him to be so attired at coroner's court hearings, but he was doing so as a mark of honour and respect for a brave young pilot who had served in 11 Group of Fighter Command – a group that Smith revealed he had also had the privilege of serving with.

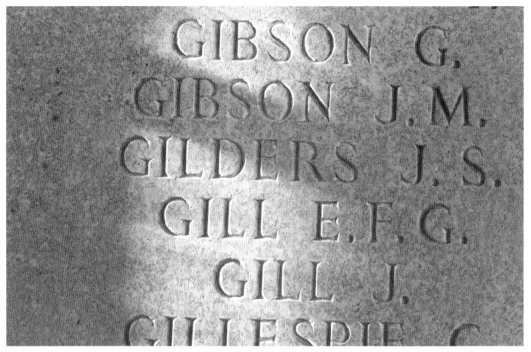

The name of John Stanley Gilders should not have appeared on the Runnymede memorial. That he was never found in 1941 is hugely unfortunate but perhaps due to the fog of war. His case was not entirely unique in that recovery of his body could so easily have been achieved at the time.

In his summing up Smith touched on legal matters and technical points surrounding such discoveries and inquests, but here is not an appropriate or relevant place to detail those issues. They have, in any case, already been dealt with in other publications. Suffice to say that Smith was, broadly speaking, seemingly supportive of what had occurred in the recovery of the gallant airman's body. On 11 May 1995 Sgt John Gilders was laid to rest in what was by now a customary military funeral at Brookwood Cemetery. It was almost the end of the saga. Almost, but not quite.

In 1996 a CWGC pattern headstone was erected over John's grave. Inexplicably it wrongly recorded John's date of death as being 21 February *1921*. It was clearly an administrative error on the part of the authorities and one that the CWGC would ultimately put right. However, it seemed symptomatic, somehow, of the almost shambolic sequence of events that had followed this brave pilot from his untimely death in 1941 to his burial in 1995.

John Gilders was the last missing Battle of Britain pilot to have been found in post-war years.

The Missing Few – An Overview

S INCE 1972 there has been a great deal of impassioned debate about the recovery of missing airmen from World War Two. Mostly this has arisen through sensationalist reporting in the news media and a degree of antagonism that developed between the authorities and the recovery groups. It is certainly the case that there have been repeat events that have hardly covered either the Ministry of Defence or those involved in recovery and research work in very much glory. Perhaps it is important to consider why this is and attempt to make a rational and balanced overview of the situation that has developed.

The RAF's Missing Research & Enquiry teams carried out sterling work across north-west Europe in the immediate post-war years identifying and laying to rest almost 20,000 airmen. It was a staggering task of epic proportions and yet the United Kingdom was not included in the work of the MREU teams. The reasons are not hard to find.

Clearly, there had been no opportunity in any way to deal with or examine the thousands of crashes in Occupied Europe or enemy territory between 1939 and 1945 and this had to be the specific focus of attention for the MREU work. In the case of the UK, of course, there must surely have been the view that all incidents involving lost RAF aircraft had been dealt with by the authorities. To an extent this was true and it is certainly the case that the crash of each aircraft involved in every casualty detailed in this book, had been known about in some way by the RAF at the time. In some cases it was certainly known who the pilot was and the specific serial number of individual aircraft had also been recorded – even if the pilot was still classed as missing.

No doubt it was the case that the RAF took the view that if a pilot was lost over the UK, then his body would have been recovered at the time of the crash *if* recovery had been in any way feasible. If he had not been recovered then, ergo, for whatever reason recovery was *not* possible. It was a logical view to take and there could be no reason, surely, why a pilot who was not recoverable in 1940 would be recoverable in 1947. Without a doubt this was the reason that sites in the UK did not come under MREU scrutiny.

With the benefit of hindsight, it is unfortunate that a more careful examination of the relatively few sites in the UK that *might* contain the mortal remains of RAF fliers did not come under more careful scrutiny by the RAF in the immediate post-war years. Had the authorities gone back and looked at their files on these cases, then many if not all of the casualties detailed in these pages might well have been struck off the missing list many years ago. In 1946 and 1947 the evidence was still much fresher. Witnesses, local police and ARP reports, evidence at the crash sites etc etc would have been easy to find and putting together the clues would have been a far less tortuous and much less complicated affair than it sometimes was for amateur researchers over forty years later. That it did not happen this way is regrettable, but a matter of fact. It would be invidious to level any criticism at the MOD (or Air Ministry as it was then) for any historical decisions that might have been taken in the late 1940s. The fact of the matter, though, was that the MOD of the 1970s and 80s inherited that situation and were singularly unprepared for the eventualities that arose.

Initially, the MOD were rather slow to react – or perhaps it was just that they felt the cases of Drake, and then Gruszka, were one-offs. Indeed, there is evidence they believed just that but as recovery work by civilian groups gathered momentum, it soon became clear that the potential for the ongoing recovery of missing airmen was far more of an issue than had previously been imagined. First, in order to attempt to regulate the situation, the MOD required that permission be sought from them for recovery but this was really only a paper exercise and did not safeguard against the discovery of a pilot's remains. Neither did it hold any weight in law.

The cases of Adair and Beresford, for example, were all carried out under MOD authority. The problem was that no historical checks were at that time made by the authorities to determine the circumstances surrounding each site. All of this changed with the introduction of the Protection of Military Remains Act in 1986 which required a formal statutory licence – only granted after detailed checks had been carried by the RAF Air Historical Branch. In cases where it was clear aircrew were still unaccounted for then a licence would not be granted because it was an already established policy of the MOD that remains should not be disturbed. To an extent, however, this legislative requirement was a case of shutting the stable door after the horse had bolted because most of the missing aircrew in the UK (and certainly from the Battle of Britain period) had already been recovered and accounted for. The emergence of the PMR Act in 1986 did little to quell either public disquiet, MOD concerns or media attention about the continuation of a state of affairs where missing aircrew might still lie within the UK and be subject either to accidental or deliberate discovery.

If the Air Ministry had got it wrong in 1946/47 it is fair to say that their successors, the Ministry of Defence, might have made errors of judgement, too. With relatively few cases to deal with might it not have been sensible for the MOD to have grasped the nettle in the 1970s and tasked its present-day maintenance units to clear up all the remaining casualties? Given that amateurs were clearly being able successfully to research, find and recover such sites (often using official records), surely it would not have been beyond the wit of the authorities to do the same? Instead, case followed upon case and with each one more confusion, embarrassment and awkwardness was heaped upon the authorities.

Angered by what was happening, and perhaps by the spotlight falling on the shortcomings of an increasingly flawed policy, the MOD directed criticism at recovery groups and individuals via the press and a degree of antipathy was understandably engendered between all parties. It was an emotive issue and emotions surely ran high. None of this helped, though, in steering a way forward with these cases.

Again, hindsight is a wonderful thing. Surely, in the light of all that had gone on, it would have been far better for amateurs and the MOD to work together in a spirit of co-operation rather than confrontation? Much could have been achieved. The careful research work conducted painstakingly by amateurs that had assembled such minute detail and the collective knowledge and experience of aviation archaeologists, would have complemented the vast resources available to the MOD and to other government agencies. Instead, the antipathy has endured right up to and including the very recent case of Flt Sgt Eric Williams. None of this has been helpful for anyone. However, what is the MOD policy, exactly, in relation to missing aircrew who are still with their aircraft?

During the late 1970s and early 1980s the position of the MOD was clear and frequently set out by the ministry when required. The head of the RAF's casualty branch A R 'Tom' Webb set the situation out in writing on 26 January 1982:

> "It has been the policy of the MOD that these remains should lie undisturbed and that the aircrew's memory should be perpetuated by the memorial at Runnymede and in the Roll of Honour at St Clement Dane's Church."

It has been a policy rigidly adhered to down the years, although in the cases of Sgt E Scott and Flt Sgt E E Williams, for example, that policy seems to have been set aside. Indeed, in more recent years there does seem to have been a shift away from the line laid down by Mr Webb. In fact, in May 2005 a spokes-person for the RAF's current casualty centre at Innsworth was quoted in the *Daily Express* in relation to a story about the discovery of a Mosquito with its two crewmembers in The Wash. She said:

> "There are some 20,000 RAF servicemen who died during the war and who don't have a grave. They are somewhere spread over Europe, maybe still in the wreckage of their aircraft. It is good that we are still finding the bodies of servicemen 60 years later because it gives the families final closure after all these years."

It was a statement very far removed from the stance adopted by the ministry in the 1970s and 80s. Again, had this been the policy then, it is likely that work to find missing aircrews would have been done officially or, at least, in a far more ordered and orderly way and with the active support of the MOD. What, though, of the Commonwealth War Graves Commission stance on such recoveries? Again, we have to go back many years (this time to 1974) to get a quote from their records officer:

> "Despite the natural reluctance to disturb human remains after such a long period of time, it must be accepted that remains left in wrecked aircraft are not secure nor are relatives or the Commission able to exercise any control over them. The Commission's policy therefore would tend to support the recovery of remains and removal to a recognised cemetery provided it were done with care and reverence."

These then have hitherto been the views set out by the authorities in the UK, although it is also interesting to note the comments of one of the world's best known and most experienced wreck recovery experts, Gerrie J Zwanenburg MBE, the retired identification & recovery officer of the Royal Netherlands Air Force. Veteran of almost countless official recoveries in the Netherlands, Zwanenburg was awarded an honorary MBE for his services towards the recovery of missing British and Commonwealth airmen. Immediately after the case involving Mark Kirby and Sgt John Gilders, Zwanenburg wrote:

> "Although it might sometimes be a difficult job to recover these aircraft and their pilots depending upon the type of crash, the nature of the soil and the terrain, I think that if it can be achieved by a young chap like Mark Kirby, as in this [Gilders] case my opinion is that it should have been done a long time ago by the official authorities."

It was a damning indictment of the enduring British policy on the subject from one who might be regarded as the world's leading expert in his field.

In setting out this book as an overview of individual cases and events, though, it is important to stress that no criticism is intended or implied of any individual MOD official – whether serving or retired. It is the policy that is the issue here, not specific MOD personnel. Indeed, it is a matter of fact that the current staff of the Historic Casework team work hard and tirelessly to ensure the many cases that arise from around the world are dealt with swiftly, efficiently and compassionately. What had gone before, especially in the 1970s and 1980s, was perhaps just a by-product of a flawed policy and a legacy of the war itself. Certainly one could legitimately question the calls of some officials in the past or query judgements that were made, but to be even-handed one could with equal legitimacy question those made by some of the recovery groups and individuals in some cases covered in this book.

In summary, it is impossible to reach anything other than an inescapable conclusion that the Ministry of Defence, and the Air Ministry before them, got things badly wrong policy-wise. For the sake of relatively few casualties, and relatively little cost or effort, the authorities could easily – and long ago – have cleared up all of the outstanding cases highlighted in this book. It would have spared much pain for all concerned.

Finally, there is one matter that must be covered and that is the role of the Commonwealth War Graves Commission in these affairs. It must be stressed that the CWGC is beyond any reproach and that their role is one *solely* of commemoration – whether through burial or memorialisation. It is not the remit of the commission to involve itself in the recovery of service casualties and they have never been equipped or required so to do. In cases where casualties have been recovered post-war, the identification of those casualties has been MOD responsibility with the duties of the CWGC extending solely to burial and commemoration and the ongoing maintenance of the burial site. Confusion as to the CWGC's role and responsibility in these cases has sometimes been apparent. It is important that where they fit into the picture is not in any way misunderstood.

What of the future? The author is not aware of any evidence that exists for additional missing Battle of Britain aircrew who might yet be found within the UK – save, that is, for those already set out in the preceding pages. This does not however preclude the possibility that evidence might yet emerge somehow to enable certain other existing burials of unknown airmen to be finally identified. Neither does it totally preclude the possibility that some accidental or unexpected recovery might yet be made that will result in the discovery of one or more hitherto missing pilots. It is the view of the author, however, that both scenarios are probably unlikely to emerge. The detailed work already carried out over more than thirty years has probably solved all of the cases that are solvable. Further, the implementation of the PMR Act and the stringent conditions that must now be satisfied before a recovery licence is granted has additionally made such future discoveries far less likely.

The moral, ethical, legal and religious ramifications are legion and complex in respect of cases relating to still missing or recently recovered aircrew. Arguments over the rights and wrongs of just about every aspect of the matter could fill a volume many times the size of this book. It has not been the purpose here to examine those issues in any detail. That has been done elsewhere by other writers. However, what cannot be ignored is that surviving next of kin in these cases have universally been relieved and comforted by the discovery of long-missing loved ones. That alone, and the reaction of relatives when confronted with such belated closure, is vindication enough that all of the recoveries charted here were right and proper. Some might not agree. I would venture to suggest that those who do not agree are largely those who are not looking at the issue from the perspective of having missing relatives. Indeed, the penultimate word ought to go to one such relative, Joan Worth, a cousin of the late Pilot Officer John Ramsay:

"The recovery of John for proper burial was undoubtedly the right thing to do. Personally, I am very greatly comforted by it. Quite frankly I find it inconceivable that these heroes should be left where they fell if there is evidence to point to where they are. Leaving them where they died cannot, surely, be an option and can only demonstrate a complete lack of any sense of history by those responsible for such matters – quite apart from any other consideration the issue ought to be given. Aside from his famous utterances on The Few, was it not Winston Churchill who said that a nation without a sense of history is a nation without a conscience, and that a nation without a conscience is a nation without a soul?"

The last word can only go to one who flew and fought during the Battle of Britain. His comments in part encapsulate what it was that inspired the author to conduct this research and to write this book:

"If I could do this one thing, could tell a little of the lives of these men, I would have justified, at least in some measure, my right to fellowship with the dead and to the friendship of those with courage and steadfastness who were still living and who would go on fighting until the ideals for which their comrades had died were stamped, forever, on the future of civilisation."
Richard Hillary, Flying Officer, Royal Air Force 1940
Killed on active service 18 January 1943

| APPENDIX I | # The Air Forces Memorial, Runnymede |

MOST OF the casualties detailed within this book are commemorated at the Commonwealth War Graves Commission Air Forces Memorial at Runnymede, erected to the memory of those members of British and Commonwealth Air Forces who were lost without trace and their graves unknown. Those lost in operations from bases in the United Kingdom and north and western Europe are remembered and in total 20,331 names are to be found here. Much has been written elsewhere about this imposing monument but given the direct connection to the casualties in this book, it would be remiss of the author not to provide the reader with a brief overview of the memorial.

The site of the Runnymede monument overlooks the River Thames and the riverside meadow where Magna Carta, enshrining man's basic freedoms under law, was sealed by King John in 1215. As such, the location resonates with symbolism in that those commemorated here died to preserve those very freedoms set down by King John so many centuries before. Indeed, when the memorial was dedicated on 17 October 1953 by HM Queen Elizabeth II, she said of those remembered here: "As only free men can, they knew the value of that for which they fought, and that the price was worth paying."

The land upon which the memorial was constructed was a gift to the nation by Sir Eugen and Lady Effie Millington-Drake in 1949 and the designing architect was Sir Edward Maufe. Principally, it comprises a shrine embraced by cloisters in which the names of the dead are recorded. These are grouped according to the year of death and of rank, inscribed on the stone reveals and mullions of the cloister giving the impression of partly opened stone books. The coats of arms of all commonwealth countries are represented on the cloister ceilings although it should be noted that as the war progressed so Britain welcomed airmen from other nations too – including the USA and occupied European countries. Casualties from some of these groups of nations may also be found remembered here.

The cloisters have curved wings terminating in two lookouts. The entrance, through a triple-arched portico, gives access to the cloisters; on the north side is the shrine, entered through a single arch with three stone figures by Vernon Hill representing Justice, Victory and Courage. Engraved on the great north window are words from Psalm 139:

If I climb up into Heaven, Thou art there;
If I go down into Hell, Thou art there also.
If I take the wings of the morning
And remain in the uttermost parts of the sea,
Even there also shall Thy hand lead me;
And Thy right hand shall hold me.

Above the angels flanking this text are engraved vapour trails taken from actual photographs of the sky during the Battle of Britain – highly appropriate given the context of this book. Of course, aircrew from the Battle of Britain form only a tiny proportion of the names recorded here and are an even smaller proportion of the staggering total of more than 116,000 men and women of the air forces of the commonwealth who were to lose their lives during World War Two.

Whilst their sacrifices were no less significant or tragic than others who died and are commemorated, it is true to say that The Few are remembered reverentially and with fondness. Of course, the names of *all* participants in the Battle of Britain are remembered individually on at least four national monuments; in Westminster Abbey, at St Clement Danes, at Capel-le-Ferne Battle of Britain Memorial and on the Battle of Britain monument on the Thames Embankment. It is only here though, at Runnymede, that the names of the missing are specifically recorded.

The design of the window and the painted ceilings of the shrine and cloisters was by

John Hutton. From the shrine, staircases lead to a gallery where a window carries verses written by Paul H Scott:

> *The first rays of the dawning sun*
> *Shall touch its pillars,*
> *And as the day advances*
> *And the light grows stronger,*
> *You shall read the names*
> *Engraved on the stone of those who sailed on the angry sky*
> *And saw harbour no more.*
> *No gravestone in yew-dark churchyard*
> *Shall mark their resting place;*
> *Their bones lie in the forgotten corners of earth and sea.*
> *But, that we may not lose their memory*
> *With fading years, their monuments stand here,*
> *Here, where the trees troop down to Runnymede.*
> *Meadow of Magna Carta, field of freedom,*
> *Never saw you so fitting a memorial,*
> *Proof that the principles established here*
> *Are still dear to the hearts of men.*
> *Here now they stand, contrasted and alike,*
> *The field of freedom's birth, and the memorial*
> *To freedom's winning.*
>
> *And, as evening comes,*
> *And mists, like quiet ghosts, rise from the river bed,*
> *And climb the hill to wander through the cloisters,*
> *We shall not forget them. Above the mist*
> *We shall see the memorial still, and over it*
> *The crown and single star. And we shall pray*
> *As the mists rise up and the air grows dark*
> *That we may wear*
> *As brave a heart as they.*

From a balcony off the gallery it is possible, on a clear day, to see seven counties. For the most part it is true to say that these include the counties over which the aircrew of RAF Fighter Command fought in 1940 and it is here, in these same counties, that the young men I have covered in this book all lost their lives. All of them are remembered at Runnymede.

When Her Majesty the Queen returned to the Runnymede memorial on 17 October 2003 to celebrate its fifty years, it also marked a period during which, one way or another, a number of the casualties remembered at this site had been accounted for. This, of course, includes those covered in *Finding The Few* as well as many more found elsewhere in Europe – principally the Netherlands during drainage and reclamation work in the Polders.

However, Her Majesty will not have found names chiselled or otherwise obliterated from the panels of the stone reveals. Indeed no. Such crude amendments would hardly be in keeping with the spirit of the place and its sanctity. Instead, it is the policy of the Commonwealth War Graves Commission to remove the names of those subsequently accounted for as and when the stone panels need renewal or replacement.

The memorial at Runnymede is a place of both pilgrimage and homage. For families it continues to be somewhere to focus the grief of loss and the burden of uncertainty still felt so many years later. Other visitors cannot fail to be moved and impressed by the monument's silent grandeur and its testimony to the inhumanity of war. Climb to the roof of the tower above the shrine, stand beneath the gold and blue crown that surmounts it and look out across the land endowed with those values that these men gave their all for. Glance down, then, at the cloistered names in serried ranks below and you will surely take in the scale of the loss remembered here. Such was the price of freedom.

The Missing Few

T HE FOLLOWING is a list of one hundred and seventy-nine aircrew of RAF Fighter Command who were lost between 10 July-31 October 1940 and who were *originally* shown as having no known grave. This is from a total casualty list of five hundred and thirty-seven Battle of Britain aircrew and thus representing exactly 33% of the overall losses – a full third of the total. In the vast majority of cases the men listed below went missing over the sea. Some may well have been recovered from the seas or coastlines around Britain and Europe and subsequently laid to rest in various locations as unknown airmen. Included in the list are those whose names it has been possible, one way or another, to remove from the official roll of missing Battle of Britain aircrew. Those men are specifically listed in italics. Each of them is covered in detail within this book.* All names shown in bold remain missing at the time of publication.

Allen J H L Fg Off	151 Sqn	12 July 1940	Buchin M S H C Plt Off	213 Sqn	15 August 1940
Andreae C J D Fg Off	64 Sqn	15 August 1940	Bulmer G G R Sub Lt	32 Sqn	20 July 1940
Arthur C J Plt Off	248 Sqn	27 August 1940	Carpenter J C Sub Lt	46 Sqn	8 September1940
Ashton D G Plt Off	266 Sqn	12 August 1940		*(Buried at sea Sept 1940)*	
	(Buried at sea Sept 1940)		Chomley J A G Plt Off	257 Sqn	12 August 1940
Baker B Sgt	264 Sqn	26 August 1940	*Clarke A W Plt Off*	*504 Sqn*	*11 September 1940*
Baker E D Sgt	145 Sqn	8 August 1940	Clarke G S Sgt	248 Sqn	1 October 1940
Beaumont W Plt Off	152 Sqn	23 September 1940	Comely P W Plt Off	87 Sqn	15 August 1940
Bennett C C Plt Off	248 Sqn	1 October 1940	Cooney C J Flt Sgt	56 Sqn	29 July 1940
Benzie J Plt Off	*242 Sqn*	*7 September 1940*	Copcut R Sgt	248 Sqn	20 October 1940
Beresford H R A Flt Lt	*257 Sqn*	*7 September 1940*	Corcoran H Sgt	236 Sqn	20 July 1940
Berry A Sgt	264 Sqn	24 August 1940	Cowsill J R Sgt	56 Sqn	13 July 1940
Bowen C E Flt Lt	607 Sqn	1 October 1940	Cox P A N Fg Off	501 Sqn	27 July 1940
Brash G B Sgt	248 Sqn	1 October 1940	Crombie R Sgt	141 Sqn	19 July 1940
Brimble J J Sgt	*73 Sqn*	*14 September 1940*	Cruttenden J Plt Off	43 Sqn	8 August 1940
Browne D O M Plt Off	1 Sqn	15 August 1940	Cunningham J L G Flt Lt	603 Sqn	28 August 1940
Bruce D C Flt Lt	111 Sqn	4 September 1940			
Brzezowski M Sgt	303 Sqn	15 September 1940	Curley A G Sgt	141 Sqn	19 July 1940
Buchanan J R Plt Off	609 Sqn	27 July 1940	*Cutts J W Fg Off*	*222 Sqn*	*4 September 1940*

D'arcy-Irvine B W J Plt Off	257 Sqn	8 August 1940
De Mancha R A Plt Off	43 Sqn	21 July 1940
Dickie W G Plt Off	601 Sqn	11 August 1940
Digby-Worsley M P Sgt	248 Sqn	19 August 1940
Doulton M D Fg Off	*601 Sqn*	*31 August 1940*
Drake G J Plt Off	*607 Sqn*	*9 September 1940*
Duszynski S Sgt	*238 Sqn*	*11 September 1940*
Dyke L A Sgt	64 Sqn	27 September 1940
Dymond W L Sgt (DFM)	111 Sqn	2 September 1940
Edworthy G H Sgt	*46 Sqn*	*3 September 1940*
Egan E J Sgt	*501 Sqn*	*17 September 1940*
Elcombe D W Sgt	602 Sqn	26 October 1940
Ellis J H M Sgt	*85 Sqn*	*1 September 1940*
Elsdon H D B Sgt	236 Sqn	18 July 1940
Eyles P R Sgt	92 Sqn	20 September 1940
Flood F W Flt Lt	235 Sqn	11 September 1940
Francis C D Plt Off	*253 Sqn*	*30 August 1940*
Gamblen D R Fg Off	41 Sqn	29 July 1940
Gillan J Fg Off	601 Sqn	11 August 1940
Gillman K R Plt Off	32 Sqn	25 August 1940
Glyde R L Fg Off (DFC)	87 Sqn	13 August 1940
Gore W E Flt Lt (DFC)	607 Sqn	28 September 1940
Green A W V Plt Off	235 Sqn	11 September 1940
Green M D Plt Off	248 Sqn	20 October 1940
Greenwood E G Sgt	245 Sqn	21 October 1940
Gruszka F Fg Off	*65 Sqn*	*18 August 1940*
Guy L N Sgt	601 Sqn	18 August 1940
Halton D W Sgt	615 Sqn	15 August 1940
Hargreaves F N Plt Off	92 Sqn	11 September 1940
Harrison J H Plt Off	145 Sqn	12 August 1940
Hawley F B Sgt	266 Sqn	15 August 1940
Haworth J F J Fg Off	43 Sqn	20 July 1940
Head F A P Sgt	236 Sqn	1 August 1940
Hewitt D A Plt Off	501 Sqn	12 July 1940
Hillcoat H B L Flt Lt	1 Sqn	3 September 1940
Hogg R M Plt Off	152 Sqn	25 August 1940
Hood H R L Sqn Ldr (DFC)	41 Sqn	5 September 1940
Horsky V Sgt	238 Sqn	26 September 1940
Howley R A Plt Off	141 Sqn	19 July 1940
Hughes D P Flt Lt (DFC)	238 Sqn	11 September 1940
Hunter P A Sqn Ldr (DSO)	264 Sqn	24 August 1940
Irving M M Flt Lt	607 Sqn	28 September 1940
Isaac L R Sgt	64 Sqn	5 August 1940
Jacobson N AC2	29 Sqn	25 August 1940
Jeff R V Flt Lt (DFC & Bar CdeG)	87 Sqn	11 August 1940
Jones J T Plt Off	264 Sqn	24 August 1940
Jottard A R I G Plt Off	145 Sqn	27 October 1940
Jowitt L Sgt	85 Sqn	12 July 1940
Kay A Sgt	248 Sqn	13 September 1940
Kay-Shuttleworth R U P (Lord) Fg Off	145 Sqn	8 August 1940
Kemp J R Plt Off	141 Sqn	19 July 1940
Kestin I H Sub Lt	145 Sqn	1 August 1940
Kidson R Plt Off	141 Sqn	19 July 1940
King F H Plt Off (DFM)	264 Sqn	24 August 1940
Kirkpatrick J C Plt Off	235 Sqn	9 October 1940
Krepski W Plt Off	54 Sqn	7 September 1940
Kwiecinski J Sgt	145 Sqn	12 August 1940
Laricheliere J E P Plt Off	213 Sqn	16 August 1940
Lee R H A Fg Off (DSO,DFC)	85 Sqn	18 August 1940
Litchfield P Plt Off	610 Sqn	18 July 1940
Little R Sgt	238 Sqn	28 September 1940
Lockton E E Sgt	236 Sqn	20 July 1940
Lukaszewicz K Fg Off	501 Sqn	12 August 1940
Macdonald D K Plt Off	603 Sqn	28 August 1940
McDonough B M Plt Off	236 Sqn	1 August 1940
Macinski J Plt Off	111 Sqn	4 September 1940
McKenzie J W Plt Off	111 Sqn	11 August 1940
McNay A L Sgt	*73 Sqn*	*5 September 1940*
Manger K Plt Off	17 Sqn	11 August 1940
Marsh H J Sgt	238 Sqn	13 August 1940
Maxwell W Sgt	264 Sqn	26 August 1940
May L D Sgt	601 Sqn	25 October 1940
Mesner B W Sgt	248 Sqn	13 September 1940
Millington W H Plt Off (DFC)	249 Sqn	30 October 1940
Mills-Smith F Sgt	601 Sqn	25 October 1940
Mitchell L R G Fg Off	257 Sqn	7 September 1940
Moody H W Plt Off	602 Sqn	7 September 1940
Moss W J M Sub Lt	213 Sqn	27 August 1940
Neville W J Sgt	610 Sqn	11 August 1940
Ostowicz A Fg Off	145 Sqn	11 August 1940
Pankratz W Flt Lt	145 Sqn	12 August 1940

Paterson P J M/Man	242 Sqn	20 August 1940
Paterson R L Plt Off	235 Sqn	18 July 1940
Peacock W A Sgt	46 Sqn	11 September 1940
Pearson G W Sgt	*501 Sqn*	*6 September 1940*
Peel C D Fg Off	603 Sqn	17 July 1940
Ponting W A Plt Off	264 Sqn	24 August 1940
Posener F H Plt Off	152 Sqn	20 July 1940
Ramsay J B Plt Off	*151 Sqn*	*18 August 1940*
Reddington L A E Sgt	152 Sqn	30 September 1940
Reece L H M Sgt	235 Sqn	18 July 1940
Rhodes R A Plt Off	29 Sqn	25 August 1940
Richardson C J Sgt	29 Sqn	31 July 1940
Ringwood E A Sgt	248 Sqn	27 August 1940
Rose-Price A T Fg Off	501 Sqn	2 September 1940
Round J H Sgt	248 Sqn	19 August 1940
Rozwadowski M Plt Off	151 Sqn	15 August 1940
Rushmer F W Flt Lt	*603 Sqn*	*5 September 1940*
Samolinski W M C Plt Off	253 Sqn	26 September 1940
Scott E Sgt	*222 Sqn*	*27 September 1940*
Sears L A Plt Off	145 Sqn	8 August 1940
Shanahan M M Sgt	1 Sqn	15 August 1940
Sharp B R Sgt	235 Sqn	11 September 1940
Shaw I G Plt Off	264 Sqn	24 August 1940
Shaw R H Plt Off	*1 Sqn*	*3 September 1940*
Shepley D C Plt Off	152 Sqn	12 August 1940
Shorrocks N B Plt Off	235 Sqn	11 September 1940
Sibley F A Sgt	238 Sqn	1 October 1940
Sim R B Sgt	111 Sqn	11 August 1940
Simpson G M Fg Off	229 Sqn	26 October 1940
Slatter D M Plt Off	141 Sqn	19 July 1940
Sly O K Sgt	29 Sqn	13 October 1940
Smith F A A/Sub/Lt	145 Sqn	8 August 1940
Smith K B Sgt	257 Sqn	8 August 1940
Steberowski M J Fg Off	238 Sqn	11 August 1940
Sterbacek J Plt Off	310 Sqn	31 August 1940
Stevens R E Sgt	29 Sqn	13 October 1940
Stocks N J Sgt	248 Sqn	20 October 1940
Stuckey S G Sgt	213 Sqn	12 August 1940
Sylvester E J H Plt Off (DFC)	501 Sqn	20 July 1940
Tucker R Y Sgt	235 Sqn	18 July 1940
Turner D E Flt Lt	238 Sqn	8 August 1940
Vinyard F F Sgt	64 Sqn	6 October 1940

Waite E Sgt	29 Sqn	31 July 1940
Wakeham C J Plt Off (DFC)	145 Sqn	8 August 1940
Walch S C Flt Lt	238 Sqn	11 August 1940
Want W H Sgt	248 Sqn	19 August 1940
Warner W H C Flt Lt	610 Sqn	16 August 1940
Warren S Sgt	1 Sqn	9 October 1940
Watts R D H Sgt	235 Sqn	11 September 1940
Weaver P S Flt Lt (DFC)	56 Sqn	31 August 1940
Westmoreland T E Sgt	616 Sqn	25 August 1940
Whitfield J J Sgt	56 Sqn	13 July 1940
Wickings-Smith P C Plt Off	235 Sqn	11 September 1940
Wildblood T S Plt Off	152 Sqn	25 August 1940
Wilkes G N Sgt	213 Sqn	12 August 1940
Williams C W Sqn Ldr	17 Sqn	25 August 1940
Williams E E Flt Sgt	*46 Sqn*	*15 October 1940*
Wilson R R Plt Off	111 Sqn	11 August 1940
Wise J F Sgt	141 Sqn	19 August 1940
Withall L C Flt Lt	152 Sqn	12 August 1940
Wojcicki A Sgt	213 Sqn	11 September 1940
Woodger D N Plt Off	235 Sqn	24 August 1940
Zenker P Plt Off	501 Sqn	24 August 1940

* Not included in this listing, although covered within the book, are Sgts H H Adair (213 Sqn, 6 November 1940) and J S Gilders (41 Sqn, 21 February 1941). Although both had been Battle of Britain pilots, they died outside the official period of the battle and thus were not officially Battle of Britain casualties.

Note: The 8 and 11 August 1940 saw the heaviest 'missing' losses with twelve pilots and aircrew unaccounted for on each of those two days alone – twenty-four men in total. Almost certainly all of these men were lost over the English Channel with these losses reflecting the heavy fighting then taking place over convoys and coastal areas and, in particular, the battles over Convoy CW9 Peewit of 8 August 1940. The lack of any adequate air-sea rescue facility doubtless contributed to the numbers who were not rescued and whose bodies would go un-recovered.

Addenda

In addition to the above listed aircrew, the following non-aircrew personnel were also lost with RAF Fighter Command between 10 July and 31 October 1940 and have no known grave. They are:

Toy E J AC2	32 MU
Ward T LAC	32 MU
Gordon D M (Mr)	Civilian

Selected Bibliography

The following books and publications were amongst those referred to by the author during the preparation of this work.

Barker, Ralph: *That Eternal Summer* (Collins, 1990)

Caldwell, Donald L: *The JG26 War Diaries* (Grub Street, 1996)

Cornwell, Peter: *Battle of France Then & Now* (Plaistow Press, 2008)

Foreman, John: *RAF Fighter Command Victory Claims* (Part Two) (Red Kite 2003)

Franks, Norman L R: *RAF Fighter Command Losses 1939-41* (Midland Publishing, 1997)

Franks, Norman L R: *Valiant Wings* (Crécy,1988)

Grabler, Josef: *Helmut Wick* (Verlag Scherl, Berlin 1941)

Gretzyngier, Robert: *Poles in Defence of Britain* (Grub Street, 2001)

Hadaway, Stuart: *Missing Believed Killed* (Pen & Sword, 2008)

Johnstone, Sandy AVM: *Enemy in the Sky* (William Kimber, 1976)

Knight, Dennis: *Harvest of Messerschmitts* (Leo Cooper, 1981)

McKee, Alexander: *Into The Blue* (Souvenir Press, 1981)

Price, Alfred: *The Hardest Day* (McDonald & Jane's, 1979)

Price, Alfred: *Battle of Britain Day* (Sidgwick & Jackson, 1990)

Ramsey, Winston: *Battle of Britain Then & Now* (Plaistow Press, 1980)

Rhodes-Moorhouse, Linda: *Kaleidoscope* (Arthur Barker, 1960)

Sarkar, Dilip: *Missing in Action:Resting in Peace?*(Ramrod, 1998)

Shaw, Frank & Joan: *We Remember The Battle of Britain* (Echo Press, 1990)

Smith, Richard C: *Hornchurch Eagles* (Grub Street, 2002)

Townsend, Peter: *Duel of Eagles* (Weidenfeld & Nicolson, 1970)

Willis, John: *Churchill's Few* (Michael Joseph, 1985)

Wynn, Kenneth G: *Men of The Battle of Britain* (CCB, 1999)

Zielinski, Jozef: *Polish Airmen in the Battle of Britain* (Oficyna Wydawnicza, 2000)

Index

Places

Airfields

RAF Squadron & Units